Poynter Institute for Media Studies Library

LITERACY:

Profiles of America's Young Adults

by Irwin S. Kirsch
and Ann Jungeblut

Poynter Institute for Media Studies
Library

FEB -9 '87

Report No. 16-PL-02

The National Assessment of Education Progress is funded by the Office for Educational Research and Improvement under a grant to Educational Testing Service. National Assessment is an education research project mandated by Congress to collect data over time on the performance of young Americans in various learning areas. It makes available information on assessment procedures to state and local education agencies.

This report, No. 16-PL-02, can be ordered from the National Assessment of Educational Progress at Educational Testing Service, Rosedale Road, Princeton, New Jersey 08541.

Library of Congress, Catalog Card Number: 86-62416

ISBN 0-88685-054-1

The work upon which this publication is based was performed pursuant to Grant No. NIE-G-84-0013 of the Office for Educational Research and Improvement. It does not, however, necessarily reflect the views of that agency.

Educational Testing Service is an equal opportunity/affirmative action employer.

Educational Testing Service, ETS, and ETS are registered trademarks of Educational Testing Service.

> "Everything should be as simple as possible; but no simpler."
> — Albert Einstein

This study inventories the literacy skills of America's young adults, ages 21-25.

By yesterday's standards the news is good:

- Ninety-five percent can read and understand the printed word.

In terms of tomorrow's needs, there is cause for concern:

- Only a very small percentage can understand complex material.

While we don't have a major *illiteracy* problem, we do need to improve the skills of most of our young adults. In other words, we do have a *literacy* problem.

This report will be a disappointment to those looking for a single number in answer to the question, "How many illiterates are there in America?"

In 1886, when signing one's name was proof of literacy, counting illiterates was a simple task. Today, the challenge is more complex. A literate person in today's America is one who can take advantage of society's opportunities and contribute to its improvement. The definition of literacy developed for this study encompasses both aspects.

What about tomorrow, with its even more demanding international and domestic environments? Will we have the human resources necessary for leadership and a competitive edge? Will our citizens be equipped to improve the quality of their lives? The data reported in this document will be of interest to employers, national defense planners, economists, sociologists, and international policymakers, as well as to educators.

It is our hope that this booklet and the database upon which it rests will enlighten the current debate on illiteracy in America. An attempt has been made to describe the results in terms that suggest remedial action. There is cause for optimism in the finding that most of us can decode printed symbols and can, therefore, use them to improve our skills.

Setting standards in America is a marvelous, informal, dynamic process that usually brings us to some consensus. Still, defining a single, clear literacy goal for our heterogeneous population with its mosaic of cultures and lifestyles is well-nigh impossible.

It's not that simple!

Archie E. Lapointe
Executive Director
NAEP

Table of Contents

	Page
Foreword..	v
Introduction...	1
Major Findings..	4
Major Conclusions...	5
Section 1 - Profiling Literacy Skills........................	7
Overview and Framework.......................................	7
The Profiles of Literacy...	8
Prose Literacy..	8
Document Literacy...	18
Quantitative Literacy.......................................	30
Section 2 - Comparing Young Adults with NAEP's In-School Population................................	38
Young Adults and and In-School 17-Year Olds............	39
Comparing Young Adults to Three Grade Levels........	40
Section 3 - Characterizing the Young Adults........	42
Age at Which English Was Learned.........................	42
Access to Literacy Materials in the Home.................	44
Levels of Parental Education.....................................	44
Young Adults' Levels of Education...........................	45
Reported Reasons for Dropping Out of High School...	47
Young Adults Who Studied for and Completed the GED	48
Current Educational Status.....................................	50
Young Adults' Occupational Status..........................	51
Current Literacy Activities.......................................	52
Section 4 - Explaining Levels of Literacy...............	54
Accounting for Racial/Ethnic Differences.................	56
Cautionary Note...	58
Section 5 - Oral Language Task Performance.......	59
The Oral Language Tasks..	59
Scoring the Oral Tasks...	60
Task Accomplishment..	60
Background Characteristics.....................................	62
Relating Oral-Task Performance to the Proficiency Scales...	62
Section 6 - Summary and Conclusions.....................	63

Foreword

Is illiteracy a major problem among young adults in the United States?

That is the major question addressed by the work summarized in this report; work that has produced the most conceptually and analytically sophisticated study of adult literacy ever conducted in this country. Now we, as readers, may judge for ourselves what the answer to the question must be.

Conceptually, this study avoids the almost universal tendency to oversimplify the nature of literacy and to divide the population into neat categories of "illiterate," "functionally illiterate," and "literate." Rather, it recognizes that people develop a variety of literacy abilities that reflect the social settings in which they interact with printed materials, whether this be the home, community, school, or workplace. The investigators in this study have produced a "profile of adult literacy" that provides four perspectives on how well young adults aged 21 through 25 years perform literacy tasks involving the use of prose materials (which predominate in home and school settings), documents (like forms, procedural guides, manuals, and so forth that are widely used in commercial and civil life in the United States), quantitative literacy materials (in which reading and mathematics are intertwined, as in reading a menu and calculating the cost of a meal), and materials used by fourth, eighth, and eleventh grade students in school.

Analyses in this report reveal that, based on the standard of "literacy" of a hundred years ago, the ability to sign one's name, virtually all young adults are "literate." If the standard of the World War II era, some 50 years ago is applied, almost 95 percent of young adults are estimated to meet or exceed the performance of fourth grade students. Based on the standard of the War on Poverty, twenty-five years ago, 80 percent of young adults meet or exceed the performance of students in the eighth grade.

But what about contemporary standards? The study's authors wisely avoid establishing arbitrary standards and recognize that that is properly the responsibility of the adult community at large. Extensive information is provided about the abilities of young adults to work with printed materials and to perform many of the information processing tasks demanded by contemporary society. And here it should be noted that a major procedural innovation was introduced: no multiple choice questions were developed for the literacy assessment. Rather, the more demanding activity of performing simulated, "real world" tasks was used to assess literacy skills. Given this emphasis upon performance, it is impressive to find that young adults correctly performed more than two-thirds of the quantitative and prose tasks, and over 80 percent of the document tasks that are so characteristic of the world of work. Is it reasonable to declare people who can perform such a wide variety of literacy tasks "illiterate" or "functionally illiterate?"

But what about those who did not perform well on the literacy assessment? This study provides a revealing analysis of just what makes a literacy task difficult. The analysis is particularly apt given the transformation that our society is making from an industrial to an "informational" economic base. The study's authors provide an "information processing" analysis of the literacy tasks and show how failure to perform correctly reflects these information processing demands. This is a signal contribution because it provides directions for instruction that go well beyond the traditional concepts of "remedial literacy" as decoding sights to sounds or producing and comprehending oral histories and the like. What this study suggests is that the performance of literacy tasks involves difficult information processing such as locating the correct information in complex displays of print, holding information in "working memory" while finding additional information, transforming these fragments of information into new knowledge, and then writing or otherwise communicating the results of these complex, cognitive activities. And frequently this will involve not just the reading of textual material, but the study of tables, graphs, and the performance of computations in order to complete a literacy task.

It is this complexity of information processing, not some simple concept of "illiteracy," that limits the performance of the "mid-level" literates that comprise some 50 percent of the young adult population. Additionally, however, for the 5 percent or so of this population who perform below the level of students in the fourth grade, and the 1 percent who did not qualify to participate in the literacy study at all, we are given insights that suggest why traditional remedial literacy programs may make so little improvement in the fifty or so hours they are able to work with students. The premise of programs that hope to make rapid and dramatic improvements in adult literacy skills is that adults have high levels of oral language abilities, and so with a few hours of training in decoding, adults would cross the threshold into the world of print and be able to bring their oral language skills to bear in comprehending the written language.

But this study reveals a disappointing fact: those adults low in literacy tend also to be low in oral language competence. This finding is presented for speaking in the present study, but it has been confirmed for listening comprehension in numerous other studies. The implication is that much longer periods of intervention are needed to make significant improvements in both the language and the literacy skills of the least literate in the nation. In turn, this suggests the need for much stronger efforts, beginning earlier in the schools, to prevent students from reaching adulthood without adequate language and literacy skills.

In an analysis designed to yield insights for intervention, the authors of this study reveal that there is a largely overlooked opportunity to improve preschool learning by a more intensive effort to educate the 3 percent or so of young adults who drop out of school before the completion of the eighth grade and who achieve only minimal literacy skills. There is a significant relationship among parents'education levels, the persistence of their children in school, and their achievement in school. This suggests that a more intensive effort to educate youth and adults who are present or future parents may produce an "intergenerational transfer" of literacy that will better prepare preschool children for school.

Finally, this study provides a focus for interventions. It is well known, and further substantiated by this study, that America is home to minority populations that are grievously overrepresented in the lowest levels of educational achievement. Because these groups are the fastest growing segments of our overall population, it follows that if something substantial is not done to increase minority achievement, the general capability of our nation's human resources will decline significantly in the coming decades. What will be done?

Is illiteracy a major problem for young adults in America? While this study does not, and indeed, given the social nature of literacy standards, could not answer this question to everyone's satisfaction, it provides information that cannot be ignored. If 5 percent of all adults lack the language and literacy skills of competent fourth grade students, as was found for this sample of 21- through 25-year olds, then it is easily the case that some ten million adults are functioning below the standards of half a century ago. This is a conservative estimate based on simple extrapolation across the full age range of adults. Yet this study did not sample military personnel living on post, street people, or institutionalized young adults such as prisoners. And we can be certain that older adults have higher rates of below fourth grade achievement.

So here we are. On the one hand we should, as a nation, celebrate Literate America, for the last century has witnessed the remarkable feat of bringing more than 95 percent of young adults to levels of literacy that exceed by far the results of the mass literacy campaigns of the Soviet Union and Cuba, in which illiteracy was declared to have been "eradicated" when the adult population reached third grade levels of achievement. By the standards of international mass literacy campaigns, the United States is a nation of literates.

Yet, by the standards of the information age, we should press harder for more rigorous education and training in the knowledge and information processing skills that now limit the flexibility of the 50 percent or so of our adults who possess "mid-level" literacy. As the need emerges to engage more often in retraining and continuing education in the face of change, lack of the skill to learn rapidly from textual materials in concentrated programs or in on-the-job learning sessions will strain the capabilities of the "mid-level" literates. What we need now are education and training programs that can develop the existing literacy skills of adults to higher levels while providing the knowledge to master the new challenges that will face today's young adults in the 21st century.

Thomas G. Sticht
Applied Behavioral & Cognitive Sciences, Inc.
San Diego, California

Introduction

> The often heard charge, "Johnny can't read," is a little like saying "Johnny can't cook." Johnny may be able to read the directions for constructing a radio kit, but not a Henry James novel, just as Johnny may be able to fry an egg but not cook Peking duck. In discussing reading in the schools, we must recognize that reading involves as wide a range of different types of texts as there are types of food. And, to imply, as does the slogan, "Johnny can't read," that reading is a single skill suited to all types of texts does not do justice to the range of reading types.
>
> Beach and Appleman in *Becoming Readers in a Complex Society,* 1984 (p. 115)

The complexity and diversity of literacy tasks in our society demand rejection of a simplistic single standard for literacy. As reflected in the quotation above, there is no single measure or specific point on a scale that separates the "literate" from the "illiterate." Scholarly discussions regarding levels of literacy have been based primarily on results from standardized reading tests and, beginning in 1970, on national surveys of literacy performance. Common to both standardized tests and the national survey measures, literacy has been treated as a fixed inventory of skills that can be defined and measured by a single test, the results of which are seen as being universally applicable to a wide range of contexts. In this framework, literacy is treated as an ability that lies along a single continuum with scores indicating the various amounts of the trait an individual possesses. Moreover, a single point is selected below which people are classified as either "illiterate" or "functionally illiterate." However, the important question facing our society today is not, "How many illiterates are there?" but rather, "What are the nature and levels of literacy skills demonstrated by various groups in the population?"

Historians have focused on two criteria as indicators of literacy rates in America before 1900: The first are counts of signatures taken from legal documents such as wills, marriage licenses, and deeds. The other is based on Census surveys beginning around 1840 in which people were simply asked whether they could read or write. After the Civil War, the focus was on tracking crude literacy rates among the emancipated Black Americans and among the growing number of European immigrants.* At that point in our history, as the Industrial Revolution was well under way and as compulsory schooling was becoming a major concern, it made sense to ask "What is the number of illiterate people in America?", because there were large numbers of individuals who had not reached even these most simple criteria.

As formal education became an integral part of our society and we became more literate, more refined indices of literacy were developed; e.g., reading grade-level scores, years of education completed, and tests of "functional literacy." Still, the focus was on the number of "illiterates" or "functional illiterates," thereby maintaining the earlier simplistic distinction. Today, the information-processing requirements associated with the broad range of materials and purposes people have for reading require that our nation's focus on literacy shift from one of "How many," to one recognizing the various types and levels of literacy characteristic of our society today. No longer can we rely on distinctions based on the simplistic notion that "literates" and "illiterates" can be neatly pigeonholed.

From this perspective, in 1985 the National Assessment of Educational Progress (NAEP) assessed the literacy skills of America's young adults. NAEP used a wide variety of tasks that simulate the diversity of literacy activities that people encounter at work, at home, at school, and in their communities. In order to take account of the many points of view that exist regarding literacy, NAEP convened panels of experts who helped set the framework for this assessment. Their deliberations led to the definition of literacy adopted:

---

*L. C. Stedman & C. F. Kaestle, *An Investigation of Crude Literacy, Reading Performance, and Functional Literacy in the United States, 1880 to 1980* (Program Report 86-2). Madison, WI: Wisconsin Center for Education Research, School of Education, University of Wisconsin-Madison, 1986.

> **Using printed and written information to function in society, to achieve one's goals, and to develop one's knowledge and potential.**

Inherent in this definition are two important distinctions. The first is that the definition rejects an arbitrary standard such as signing one's name, completing five years of school, or scoring at the eighth-grade level on a test of reading achievement. Second, following from the work of William S. Gray in the 1950s and national literacy surveys of the 1970s, it implies a set of complex information-processing skills that go beyond decoding and comprehending textual materials.

To conduct this assessment, NAEP drew a nationally representative household sample of 21- to 25-year-olds living in the 48 contiguous United States. Some 40,000 households were contacted to locate and assess approximately 3,600 young adults. The assessment was conducted by some 500 interviewers, and each interview lasted about 90 minutes. Approximately 60 of the 90 minutes were devoted to measuring proficiencies on tasks that simulate those encountered in various adult settings, such as:

- **reading and interpreting prose, as in newspaper articles, magazines, and books;**
- **identifying and using information located in documents such as forms, tables, charts, and indexes; and,**
- **applying numerical operations to information contained in printed material such as a menu, a checkbook, or an advertisement.**

The remaining 30 minutes were devoted to obtaining background information that could be related to performance on the simulation tasks. Questions focused on the respondent's current reading and writing activities, occupational status and aspirations, educational and early language experiences, and home characteristics.

The information obtained from these interviews is compiled on a data tape that is available to the public, as is the full Final Report of this assessment.* The Final Report presents a more detailed account of the assessment procedures, findings, and conclusions than does this document. This national database provides the most recent and complete picture of the literacy skills and practices of America's young adults.

---

*I. Kirsch & A. Jungeblut. *Literacy: Profiles of America's Young Adults, Final Report* (Report No. 16-PL-01). Princeton, N.J.: National Assessment of Educational Progress, 1986.

NAEP's decision to focus its attention on our country's approximately 21 million young adults aged 21-25 recognizes the importance of this population because they are among the most recent entrants into the labor force and yet represent (after teenagers) the largest proportion of unemployed in this country. Perhaps more important, projections indicate that the composition of this young-adult population will change in important ways over the next decade. The total number of individuals aged 21 to 25 is expected to decrease from around 21 million to 17 million, but the total group will include a larger proportion of minority group members.

NAEP characterized the literacy skills of America's young adults in terms of three "literacy scales" representing distinct and important aspects of literacy:

- **prose literacy** — the knowledge and skills needed to understand and use information from texts that include editorials, news stories, poems, and the like;

- **document literacy** — the knowledge and skills required to locate and use information contained in job applications or payroll forms, bus schedules, maps, tables, indexes, and so forth; and,

- **quantitative literacy** — the knowledge and skills needed to apply arithmetic operations, either alone or sequentially, that are embedded in printed materials, such as in balancing a checkbook, figuring out a tip, completing an order form, or determining the amount of interest from a loan advertisement.

Simulation tasks representing each of the three literacy scales are described on the basis of task characteristics that relate to the complexity of the processes required for successful performance and not by the vocabulary or sentence length of the printed material. In addition, results for young adults are also presented on a fourth scale: the reading proficiency scale developed by NAEP to report results from its 1983-84 reading assessment. Exercises from the NAEP reading scale were included to link the performance of young adults to that of NAEP's in-school population.

Major Findings

▶ The literacy problem identified for the nation's young adults can be characterized in two ways: While the overwhelming majority of young adults adequately perform tasks at the lower levels on each of the three scales, sizable numbers appear unable to do well on tasks of moderate complexity. Only a relatively small percentage of this group is estimated to perform at levels typified by the more complex and challenging tasks.

- Inevitably, smaller percentages of young adults are found to perform at increasing levels of proficiency on each of the scales. The fact that fewer and fewer individuals attain these moderate and high levels of proficiency is most pronounced for young adults who terminate their education early and for minority group members.

- Black young adults, on average, perform significantly below White young adults — by almost a full standard deviation. Hispanic young adults, on average, perform about midway between their Black and White peers. These differences appear at each level of education reported.

- Nearly half of the White and Hispanic young adults who enrolled in a GED (General Educational Development) program went on to attain the credential, compared with less than one-fourth of the Black young adults.

- Home-support variables (such as parents' education and access to literacy materials) were found to be significantly related to the type and amount of education and to the literacy practices reported by young adults. These, in turn, help to explain differences in literacy-skill levels.

- On average, young adults perform significantly better on the NAEP reading scale than do in-school 17-year-olds. This suggests that further education and participation in society contribute to the improvement of reading skills represented by that scale.

- Only about two percent of this young-adult population were estimated to have such limited literacy skills that it was judged that the simulation tasks would unduly frustrate or embarrass them. Roughly one percent (or about half) of this group reported being unable to speak English.

- The English-speaking one percent, instead of attempting the simulation tasks, responded to a set of oral-language tasks. The comparatively low performance indicates that this group (about 225,000 people) may have a language problem that extends beyond processing printed information.

These findings and others to be discussed in this report have implications for program planning and policy decisions, as do the major conclusions highlighted here.

Major Conclusions

- It is clear from these data that "illiteracy" is not a major problem for this population. It is also clear, however, that "literacy" *is* a problem. Sizable numbers of individuals are estimated to perform within the middle range on each of the scales. Within these broad ranges, individuals are neither totally "illiterate" nor fully "literate" for a technologically advanced society.

▶ The overwhelming majority of America's young adults are able to use printed information to accomplish many tasks that are either routine or uncomplicated. It is distressing, however, that relatively small proportions of young adults are estimated to be proficient at levels characterized by the more moderate or relatively complex tasks. It has been argued that many, if not most, of society's managerial, professional, and technical service-sector jobs will require participation in some postsecondary program. This argument raises the question of whether or not individuals with more limited literacy skills will qualify for or benefit from such education and training programs.

▶ As a society, we will have to develop and apply appropriate intervention strategies to meet the diverse needs of these young adults. Strategies must be tailored not only to help those whose literacy skills are most limited, but also to upgrade the literacy skills of those who demonstrate low to moderate levels of proficiencies. In addition, we must find ways to expand the number of those in our population who are able to perform society's more challenging tasks.

▶ The relatively poor performance of minority group members and those who terminated their education early, combined with the projected changes in demographics for the 21- to 25-year-old population, suggest that unless we develop and implement more appropriate intervention and prevention strategies, America will have a less literate pool of young adults to fill its human resource needs over the next decade or so.

▶ To the extent that the skills identified in this literacy study are important for full participation in our society, this assessment raises questions about whether we should seek better ways to teach the current curriculum or whether we need to reconsider what is taught as well as how we teach it.

▶ It is clear that there is no single step or simple action, which if taken, will allow all individuals to become fully literate. Becoming literate in our society is a lifelong pursuit affected by such factors as home environment, economic situation, aspirations, opportunities, and education. As a result, we must recognize the intergenerational effects on literacy.

The following sections highlight major aspects of the assessment. Included are an overview of the assessment and profiles of the estimated literacy proficiencies of young adults, comparisons of young adults with in-school 17-year-olds regularly assessed by NAEP, characteristics of the young adults, relationships of background characteristics to performance on the proficiency scales, a description of the oral language results for selected samples of this population, and a final section providing a summary and conclusions.

Section 1

Profiling Literacy Skills

Overview and Framework

The design of NAEP's young adult literacy assessment was based on the recognition that literacy is inextricably linked with home, school, work, and social environments. To gain a better and deeper understanding of the condition of literacy among 21- to 25-year-olds in America, it followed that information relating to early background and current environment would be of paramount importance. So much so that 30 of the 90 minutes planned for the assessment interview were devoted to questions covering such demographic characteristics of young adults as the environments in which they grew up, their early language experiences, their educational attainment and aspirations, their employment status, their current reading and writing activities, and their involvement in community affairs.

The second phase involved the measurement of "core" skills. The core served to identify individuals with limited skills who, when faced with the simulation tasks, would very likely be frustrated and embarrassed. The third phase of the assessment consisted of two components. An oral language interview was administered to those individuals judged to have extremely limited literacy skills on the basis of their performance on the core tasks and to a random sample of the individuals who were administered the simulation tasks. The remaining, and key, component of this phase of the assessment included a broad range of simulation tasks.

The simulation tasks represent a variety of purposes people have for using printed material and the variety of the materials associated with these purposes. This framework was applied to task development because it takes into account the growing body of research that recognizes performance on a given task is in part determined by what the reader is expected to do with printed material (use) and not simply the material itself. The more than 100 literacy tasks were organized into three scales — quantitative literacy, document literacy, and prose literacy. The prose tasks subsequently were divided into two scales: the

NAEP in-school, multiple-choice exercises and the simulation tasks developed for the assessment. By organizing the tasks in this way, NAEP is able to profile the proficiencies of young adults on four scales.

The Profiles of Literacy

Each of the proficiency scales extends from 0-500 with a mean of 305 and a standard deviation of about 50.* Both tasks and individuals can be placed along a particular scale, thereby providing a means for describing various levels of proficiency. To interpret levels of proficiency, tasks at selected points are described and illustrated in order to identify characteristics that exemplify the complexity of processing required for successful performance at these various levels.

The results described in this report are representative of the roughly 21 million young adults, 21- to 25-years old, residing in households. About two percent of this population, or approximately 440,000 young adults, were judged to have such limited literacy skills that they were not administered the simulation tasks. Slightly more than half of this two percent, or about 225,000, were estimated to be Spanish-speaking. Due to the relatively small number of observations for this group (two percent), the literacy profiles are based on the 98 percent of this sample who are English-speaking and who responded to the printed simulation tasks. Approximately 77 percent of the group who responded to the simulation tasks are estimated to be White, 13 percent Black, 6 percent Hispanic and, 4 percent of other racial/ethnic origins.

Prose Literacy

An important aspect of literacy is the knowledge and skills needed to understand and use information contained in various kinds of textual material. The prose scale represents three qualitatively different aspects of reading comprehension. Each of these aspects, in turn, extends over a range of difficulty.

1. **Locating information in text.** Readers who successfully perform these tasks match information given in the form of a question with either identical or corresponding information stated in text. The simplest task requires the reader to match information in a question with information in a text on the basis of a single, commonly shared feature. The most complex task requires the reader to match on the basis of *three* categories of information that are not identically phrased in the question and the material.

---

*The performance of young adults was linked to the NAEP reading scale. Average proficiency on the three literacy scales was set equal to the average proficiency of 305 for the adults on the NAEP scale.

2. **Producing and interpreting text information.** Readers successfully performing these tasks use background knowledge or a combination of background and text information to produce a response that supports a statement or idea given in a question. The least complex task of this type asks the reader to write a brief description of a job that he or she would like to have. The most complex task requires the reader to use information from a text to talk about the differences between two categories of work-related fringe benefits.

3. **Generating a theme or organizing principle from text information.** Readers who successfully perform these tasks synthesize information to generate a theme or organizing principle that is consistent with the arguments provided in a text. The most simple task of this type involves generating the theme of a poem that uses several familiar metaphors to imply the theme of "war." A somewhat more difficult task requires the reader to synthesize the main argument of a lengthy newspaper column.

TABLE 1

Selected Tasks and Corresponding Levels of Difficulty Defining the Three Aspects of the Prose Comprehension Scale

Selected Prose Comprehension Tasks

Levels of Difficulty	Matching Literal and Corresponding Information	Producing and Interpreting Text	Generating a Theme
500			
400	(397)* Three-feature match from newspaper article (corresponding)		(387)* Generate theme from single unfamiliar metaphor
375		(371)* Interpret job-related benefit classification	
350			
325			(340)* Generate theme from repetitive argument widely dispersed
300			
275	(281)* Three-feature match from a page of text in an almanac (literal)	(279)* Interpret appliance warranty	(278)* Generate familiar theme from repetitive argument
250			
225			
200	(210)* One-feature match from newspaper article (corresponding)	(199)* Produce text with personalized background	
0			

*Designates that point on the scale at which individuals with that level of proficiency have an 80 percent probability of responding correctly.

Table 1 shows that across a broad range of the prose scale successful performance is associated with the strategies appropriate for each of the three aspects of reading identified. This table also highlights the fact that there is significant overlap among the estimated difficulties of tasks representing the three aspects of prose comprehension, which suggests that tasks requiring feature matching can be as complex as those requiring the reader to interpret text and generate a theme from it.

The tasks selected to typify performance at any specified point on a scale distinguish among individuals who, at that proficiency level, have a high probability of success on those tasks as compared with individuals estimated to be at lower levels on the scale. In this assessment, the criterion for success was 80 percent probability. This means that individuals estimated to be at a given level on the scale consistently — that is, with 80 percent probability — perform tasks like those used to illustrate performance at that level. Individuals at lower levels on the scale also have a chance of successfully performing the more difficult tasks, but their probability of success is considerably lower than 80 percent and, thus, one has much less confidence that they will perform the more difficult tasks consistently. As a result, they are *not* estimated to be performing at the higher level(s) even though they occasionally succeed on more difficult tasks.

Estimates of the percentages of various groups at or above particular points of interest on the prose scale are given on the next few pages. These are points at which there are shifts in task characteristics. Selected tasks typifying these points are shown. The percentages given are for selected points on the scale and not for the individual tasks. This is because most of the selected tasks are not at the specific point, but bracket or fall on either side of it.

200 Level: 96% of Total Group

Two tasks characteristic of performance at the 200 level on the prose literacy scale are: writing a simple description of the type of job one would like to have (199), and accurately locating a single piece of information (single-feature match) from a newspaper article of moderate length (210) similar to that shown below. The question directs the reader to locate and underline the statement that indicates what the swimmer ate to keep up her strength during the swim.

Swimmer completes Manhattan marathon

The Associated Press

NEW YORK—University of Maryland senior Stacy Chanin on Wednesday became the first person to swim three 28-mile laps around Manhattan.

Chanin, 23, of Virginia, climbed out of the East River at 96th Street at 9:30 p.m. She began the swim at noon on Tuesday.

A spokesman for the swimmer, Roy Brunett, said Chanin had kept up her strength with "banana and honey sandwiches, hot chocolate, lots of water and granola bars."

Chanin has twice circled Manhattan before and trained for the new feat by swimming about 28.4 miles a week. The Yonkers native has competed as a swimmer since she was 15 and hoped to persuade Olympic authorities to add a long-distance swimming event.

The Leukemia Society of America solicited pledges for each mile she swam.

In July 1983, Julie Ridge became the first person to swim around Manhattan twice. With her three laps, Chanin came up just short of Diana Nyad's distance record, set on a Florida-to-Cuba swim.

(Reduced from original copy.)

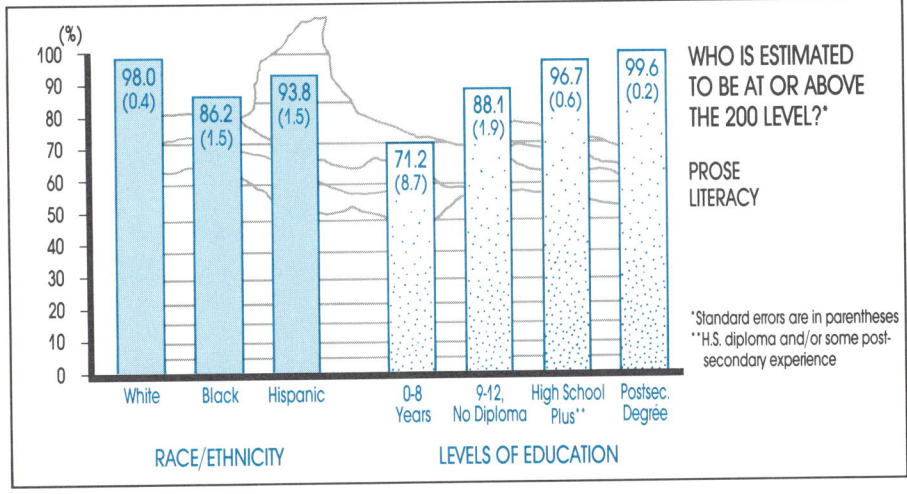

WHO IS ESTIMATED TO BE AT OR ABOVE THE 200 LEVEL?*

PROSE LITERACY

*Standard errors are in parentheses
**H.S. diploma and/or some post-secondary experience

275 Level: 72% of Total Group

Tasks characteristic of performance at the 275 level include writing a letter to explain that an error has been made in a billing charge (277); generating the theme of a poem containing numerous allusions to a familiar theme — war (278); and, interpreting the instructions from an appliance warranty to select the most appropriate description of what is wrong (279).

A manufacturing company provides its customers with the following instructions for returning appliances for service:

> When returning appliance for servicing, include a note telling as clearly and as specifically as possible what is wrong with the appliance.

A repair person for the company receives four appliances with the following notes attached. Circle the letter next to the note which best follows the instructions supplied by the company.

A. The clock does not run correctly on this clock radio. I tried fixing it, but I couldn't.

C. The alarm on my clock radio doesn't go off at the time I set. It rings 15-30 minutes later.

B. My clock radio is not working. It stopped working right after I used it for five days.

D. This radio is broken. Please repair and return by United Parcel Service to the address on my slip.

(Reduced from original copy.)

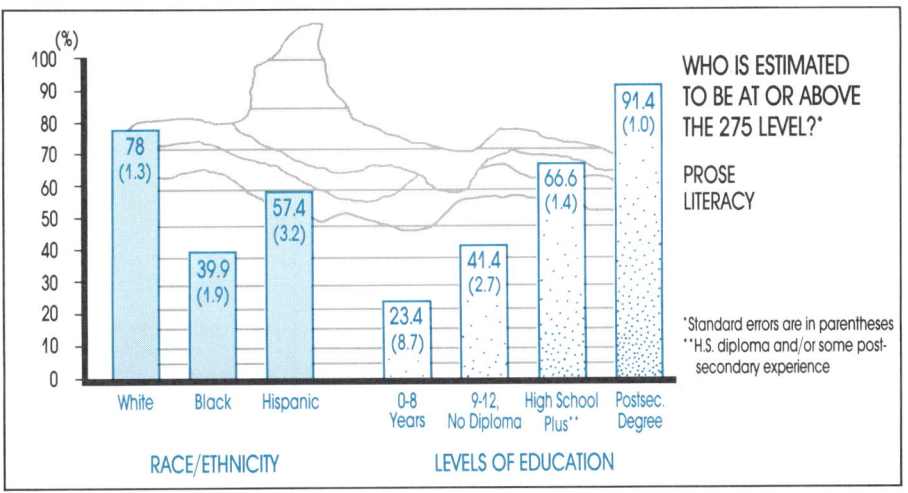

325 Level: 37% of Total Group

Bracketing the 325 level are tasks requiring the reader to locate information on the basis of three features (313) that are repeated throughout a lengthy news article or to synthesize the main argument from a lengthy newspaper column (340), the text of which is shown below.

Did U.S. know Korean jet was astray?

Tom Wicker

THE COMPLICITY with government into which the press has sunk since Vietnam and Watergate has seldom been more visible than on the first anniversary of Soviet destruction of Korean Air Lines Flight 007.

On Sept. 1, headlines, of course, reported the Reagan administration's statements that the event had boosted, during the year, U.S. standing in the world relative to that of the U.S.S.R.

But the press effectively ignored an authoritative article in The Nation (for Aug. 18-25) establishing to a reasonable certainty that numerous U.S. government agencies knew or should have known, almost from the moment Flight 007 left Anchorage, Alaska, that it was off course and headed for intrusion into Soviet air space, above some of the most sensitive Soviet military installations.

Yet no agency, military or civilian, warned Flight 007 or tried to guide it out of danger; neither did the Japanese. As late as Aug. 28, in a briefing, a State Department spokesman claimed "no agency of the U.S. government even knew the plane was off course and was in difficulty until after it was shot down."

If that's true, the author of The Nation's article—David Pearson, an authority on the Defense Department's World Wide Military Command and Control System, who spent a year researching his lengthy article—concludes, "the elaborate and complex system of intelligence, warnings and security that the U.S. has built up over decades suffered an unprecedented and mind-boggling breakdown."

But Pearson shows in excruciating detail why it's most unlikely there was any such "simultaneous failure of independent intelligence systems" of the Navy, Army, Air Force, National Security Agency, Central Intelligence Agency "or the Japanese self-defense agency"—all of which, he shows, had ability to track Flight 007 at various stages across the Pacific.

What's the alternative to the staggering idea of such a breakdown? That all these agencies deliberately chose not to guide the airliner back on a safe course, because its projected overflight of the Kamchatka Peninsula and Sakhalin Island would activate Soviet radar and air defenses and thus yield a "bonanza" of intelligence information to watching and listening U.S. electronic devices. Despite all administration protests to the contrary, the evidence Pearson presents raises this alternative at least to the high probability level.

But Pearson does not assert as a fact that the United States, South Korea or both deliberately planned an intelligence mission for Flight 007; he concedes the possibility that it simply "blundered" into sensitive Soviet air space, and that electronic onlookers for the United States decided on the spot to take intelligence advantage of the error—never dreaming the Russians would shoot down an unarmed airliner.

But if the disaster happened that way, Pearson notes, two experienced pilots (nearly 20,000 flying hours between them) not only made an error in setting the automatic pilot but "sat in their cockpit for five hours, facing the autopilot selector switch directly in front of them at eye level, yet failed to see that it was set improperly." Nor in all that time could they have used the available radar and other systems to check course and position.

Pearson also presents substantial evidence that Soviet radar detection and communications systems over Kamchatka and Sakhalin were being jammed that night, which would help account for their documented difficulty in catching up to Flight 007. He reconstructs electronic evidence too, to show that the airliner changed course slightly after passing near a U.S. RC-135 reconnaissance plane; otherwise it would have crossed Sakhalin far north of the point where a Soviet fighter finally shot it down.

The jamming and course change, as detailed by Pearson, strongly suggest what he obviously fears: "that K.A.L. 007's intrusion into Soviet airspace, far from being accidental, was well orchestrated," with the Reagan administration, at some level, doing the orchestrating. Even if not, the deliberate silence—or shocking failure—of so many U.S. detection systems argue that President Reagan and the security establishment have greater responsibility for Flight 007's fate than they admit—or that a complaisant press has been willing to seek.

Copyright 1984 by The New York Times Company. Reprinted by permission.

(Reduced from original copy)

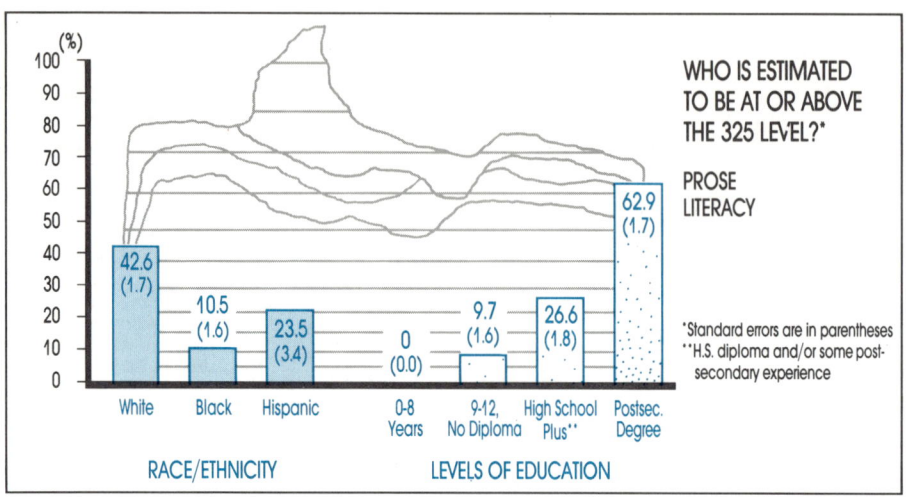

375 Level: 9% of Total Group

Tasks bracketing the 375 level on the prose scale require the reader to use text information to describe orally the distinctions between two types of employee fringe benefits (371) and to generate an unfamiliar theme from a short poem (387), as in the following example.

12. What is the poet trying to express in this poem? _____

_____

_____

_____

    The pedigree of honey
    Does not concern the Bee —
    A clover, any time, to him
    Is Aristocracy —   (Emily Dickinson)

(Reduced from original copy.)

Reprinted by permission of the publishers and the Trustees of Amherst College from *The Poems of Emily Dickinson*, edited by Thomas H. Johnson, Cambridge, Mass.: The Belknap Press of Harvard University Press, Copyright 1951, © 1955, 1979, 1983 by the President and fellows of Harvard College.

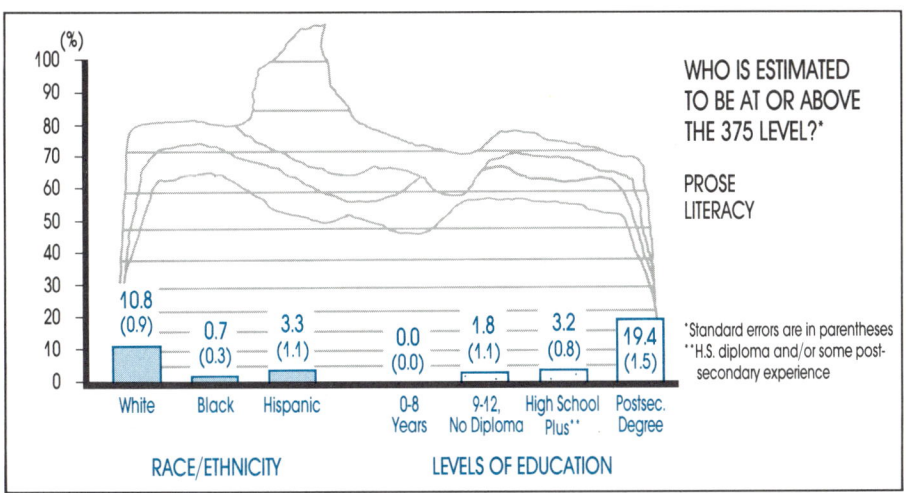

Summarizing Levels of Proficiency on the Prose Scale. It is indeed encouraging to find that most of the young adults are estimated to perform at or above the 200 level. In this assessment, tasks characteristic of this level involved locating a single fact in a news article and writing a brief description of a job one would like to have. All but four in 100 young adults are estimated to have these rather low-level literacy skills — still, almost 14 in 100 Black and six in 100 Hispanic young adults fail to achieve this level. Lack of proficiency at this level is particularly noteworthy for those with 0 to 8 years of education, where almost 30 in 100 are estimated to be below the 200 level.

At the higher levels on the prose literacy scale, the tasks become increasingly complex. It is at about the 275 level that differences among various groups become pronounced. Tasks characteristic of performance here involve writing a letter explaining an error on a credit-card bill, interpreting instructions on an appliance warranty, and generating a relatively familiar theme from a poem. While eight out of 10 White young adults are estimated to perform at or above this 275 level, only four in 10 Black and six in 10 Hispanic young adults attain this level or higher. More alarming is the fact that although nine in 10 young adults with postsecondary degrees attain this or higher levels, less than half of those with some high school experience and only one quarter of those with up to eight years of elementary schooling reach or exceed this moderate level of proficiency. It should be remembered that the 275 level is still below the overall average performance of 305.

At the 325 level of proficiency, there are many fewer young adults from all groups. Tasks typical of this level are relatively complex. They involve locating and matching information on the basis of three features from lengthy text as well as summarizing the main argument from a lengthy news column. Fewer than four in 10 young adults are estimated to attain this level — about four in 10 White, one in 10 Black,

Percentages of People and Selected Tasks At or Above Successive Points on the Prose Scale*

	Selected Tasks at Decreasing Levels of Difficulty**	Selected Points on the Scale	Total
		500	
397	Identify appropriate information in lengthy newspaper column		
387	Generate unfamiliar theme from short poem	375	8.8 (0.7)
371	Orally interpret distinctions between two types of employee benefits		
361	Select inappropriate title based on interpretation of news article	350	21.1 (1.1)
340	State in writing argument made in lengthy newspaper column		
339	Orally interpret a lengthy feature story in newspaper	325	37.1 (1.6)
313	Locate information in a news article	300	56.4 (1.5)
281	Locate information on a page of text in an almanac (3-feature)		
279	Interpret instructions from an appliance warranty		
278	Generate familiar theme of poem		
277	Write letter to state that an error has been made in billing	275	71.5 (1.4)
262	Locate information in sports article (2-feature)	250	82.7 (1.2)
		225	90.8 (0.7)
210	Locate information in sports article (1-feature)		
199	Write about a job one would like	200	96.1 (0.5)
		175	98.5 (0.2)
		150	99.7 (0.1)
		0	

**Number indicating difficulty level designates that point on the scale at which individuals with that level of proficiency have an 80 percent probability of responding correctly.

TABLE 2

Race/Ethnicity			Levels of Education			
White	Black	Hispanic	0-8 Years	9-12 Years	H.S. Diploma and/or More‡	2- or 4-Yr. Deg. or More
10.8 (0.9)	0.7 (0.3)	3.3 (1.1)	0.0 (0.0)	1.8 (1.1)	3.2 (0.8)	19.4 (1.5)
24.9 (1.3)*	3.1 (0.6)	12.0 (3.2)	0.0 (0.0)	3.8 (1.5)	12.2 (1.3)	40.3 (2.0)
42.6 (1.7)	10.5 (1.6)	23.5 (3.4)	0.0 (0.0)	9.7 (1.6)	26.6 (1.8)	62.9 (1.7)
63.2 (1.4)	23.7 (1.6)	41.1 (4.1)	12.2 (9.5)	25.1 (2.8)	48.4 (1.7)	80.5 (1.3)
78.0 (1.3)	39.9 (1.9)	57.4 (3.2)	23.4 (8.7)	41.4 (2.7)	66.6 (1.4)	91.4 (1.0)
88.0 (1.0)	57.5 (2.7)	72.1 (2.6)	27.0 (8.3)	58.7 (3.4)	81.4 (1.3)	96.1 (0.5)
94.6 (0.6)	73.6 (2.3)	80.8 (2.3)	53.7 (7.7)	73.0 (2.1)	91.2 (0.9)	98.8 (0.3)
98.0 (0.4)	86.2 (1.5)	93.8 (1.5)	71.2 (8.7)	88.1 (1.9)	96.7 (0.6)	99.6 (0.2)
99.4 (0.2)	94.1 (0.9)	96.6 (1.2)	91.8 (3.1)	93.5 (1.1)	99.0 (0.2)	99.9 (0.1)
100.0 (0.0)	97.7 (0.5)	99.8 (0.2)	97.1 (1.4)	98.7 (0.4)	99.7 (0.1)	100.0 (0.0)

*Numbers in parentheses are estimated standard errors.
‡High school diploma and/or some postsecondary experience.

and two in 10 Hispanic young adults. Even more telling is the fact that almost three in ten young adults with a high school diploma or some postsecondary experience are proficient at this level, compared with only one in 10 young adults who have some high school experience.

The tasks illustrative of the 375 level are among the most demanding prose tasks in this assessment. It is interesting to note the sharp decrease in the percentages of various groups estimated to be proficient at this level. More than 50 percent are at the 300 level but only about 9 percent performed at the 375 level. Less than one in 100 Black, only about three in 100 Hispanic, and only 11 in 100 White young adults are estimated to be at this level.

Table 2 summarizes the proficiencies of young adults on the prose literacy tasks. The percentages shown suggest that while most of the young adults in America are estimated to have attained levels of proficiency defined by tasks up to the 250 level, too many are estimated not to reach higher levels of proficiency (275-375). This fact is most notable among minority groups and those with limited education. Far too few young adults in all groups are projected to have the highest levels of prose proficiency.

Document Literacy

An important aspect of the literacy assessment was measuring the proficiencies of young adults at using documents such as indexes, tables, charts, paycheck stubs, checks, deposit slips, order forms, labels, and television listings. These tasks are not only important in our personal lives but, for many, these tasks are a necessary part of managing a household and meeting job requirements.

Analyses of the tasks making up the document scale show that one aspect of the prose scale — matching features or categories of information — seems also to be critical for successful completion of document tasks. The moderate correlation (.55) between the prose and document scales suggests, however, that other skills and strategies are also important. These probably involve procedural knowledge such as that required to complete a check or fill out an order form, to understand the hierarchical structure of indexes, as well as skills and strategies for transferring information from one document to another.

As on the prose scale, the tasks making up the document scale form a continuum of difficulty. The tasks become more difficult as:

- the number of features or categories of information the reader has to locate in the document increases;
- the number of categories of information in the document that can serve as distractors (or plausible right answers) increases; and,
- the information asked for in the question has less obvious identity with the information stated in the document.

As extreme examples, the least demanding task on this scale asked the respondent to write her or his name on the appropriate line of a social security card. Several characteristics combine to make this task easy. First, the individual is asked to provide personal background knowledge. Second, there is only one feature or category that must be matched — the individual's name to the line designated "signature." Third, there is only one place on the social security card where the individual may respond. In contrast, a much more demanding task asks the reader to locate and match six features or categories of information using a bus schedule. If the reader leaves out or forgets one of these categories, he or she is likely to respond incorrectly. In addition, there are many distractors or pieces of information that could be considered correct.

150 Level: 99.7% of Total Group

Tasks bracketing the 150 level of proficiency include signing one's name on the social security card (110), locating the expiration date on a driver's license (160), and identifying the correct time of a meeting from a form (169). The distinguishing characteristic in these latter two tasks appears to be that the information is not derived from personal background knowledge. Otherwise, each of these two tasks requires the reader to match a single feature of information that is given in both the question and the document.

For example, using the meeting room form below, respondents were directed to enter the "time" of the meeting in a space provided.

HOSPITAL MEDICAL CENTER
STAFF EDUCATION DEPARTMENT

Program **Nurses Convention — Red Bud Room**

Person In Charge **Mrs. Mathews**

Day **Tuesday**   Date **July 10**   Time **1:00 p.m.**

Number Expected **35**

A.V. Material
- Slide projector
- Screen
- Small table for projector

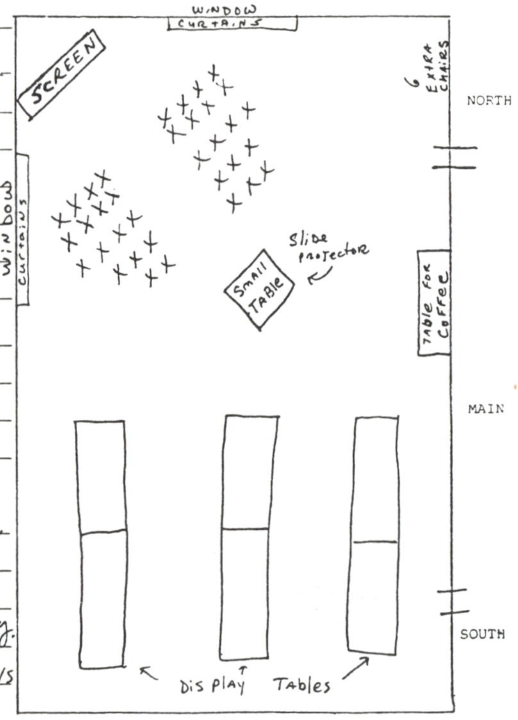

Comments

Need 6 extra chairs.

Make sure curtains close all the way.

6 Tables For Displays

1 Table For Coffee

(Room diagram shows: Screen (NW corner), Window Curtains (N and W), 6 Extra Chairs (NE), Table for Coffee (E), seating marked with x's, Small Table with Slide Projector in center, Display Tables at south end. Labeled NORTH, MAIN, SOUTH.)

(Reduced from original copy.)

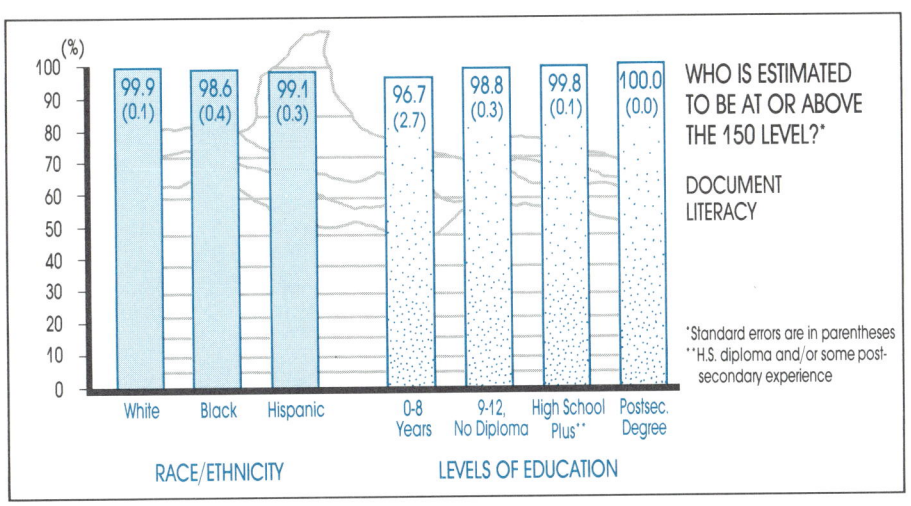

200 Level: 96% of Total Group

Tasks around this level of proficiency require the reader to engage in successive one-feature matching. For example, one question directs the reader to match money-saving coupons to a shopping list of several items (211). A slightly easier task involves entering personal background information on a job application (196). Also at about this level, we see the first task requiring a two-feature match — the reader is directed to circle the movie that comes on a particular channel at a specified time (192).

SHOPPING LIST

    milk
    instant coffee
    bread
    cake mix
    margarine
    hamburger
    eggs
    potato chips

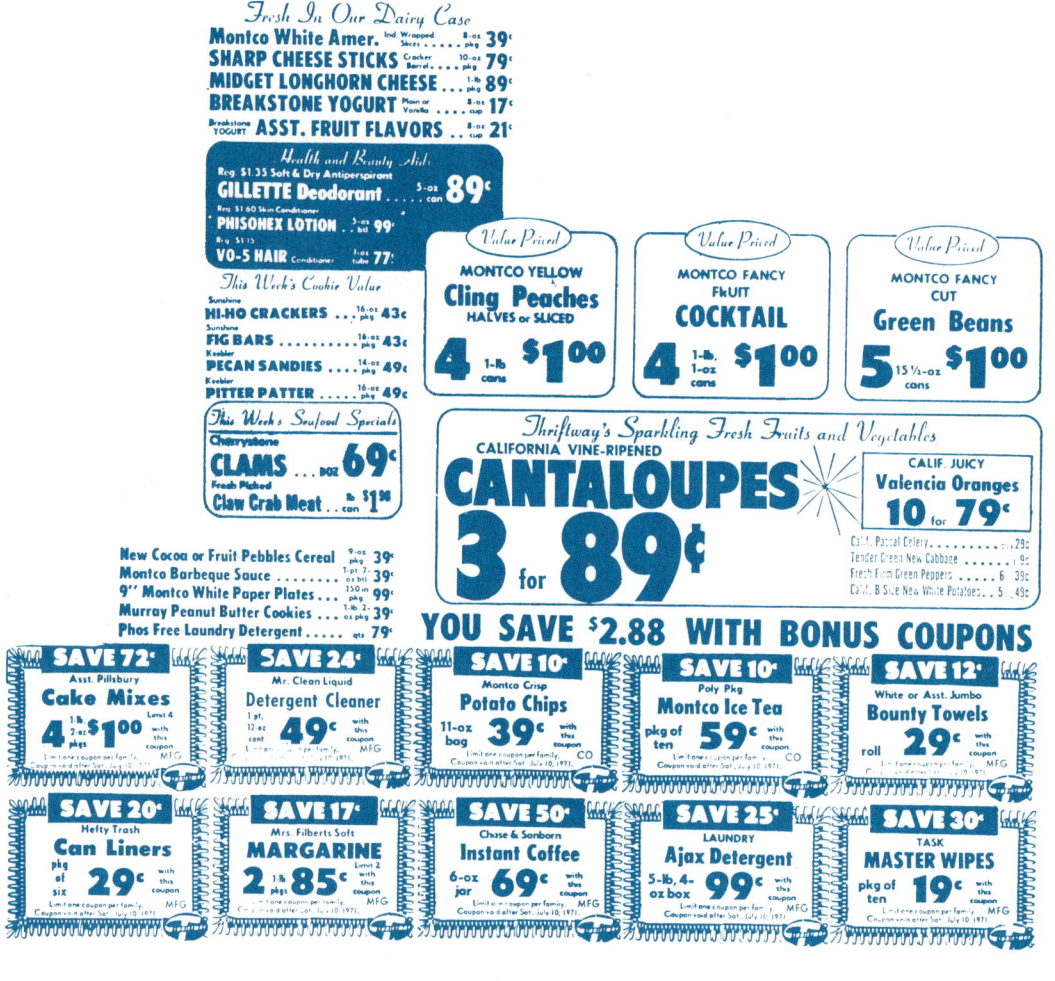

(Layout was revised slightly from the assessment to accommodate this report.)

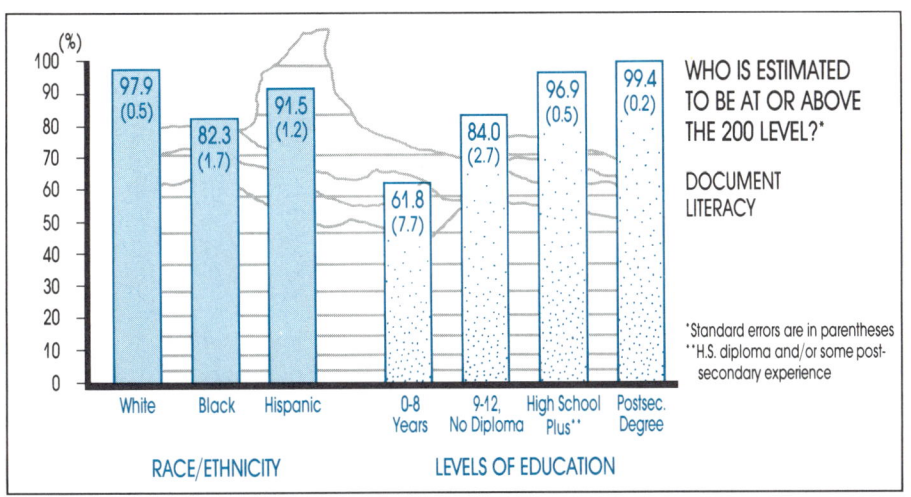

WHO IS ESTIMATED TO BE AT OR ABOVE THE 200 LEVEL?*

DOCUMENT LITERACY

*Standard errors are in parentheses
**H.S. diploma and/or some post-secondary experience

250 Level: 84% of Total Group

Tasks estimated to be at about the 250 level involve matching information on the basis of two features from documents containing several distractors or plausible answers. One such task involves locating in a table how soon an employee will be *eligible* for a particular *type* of fringe benefit (262). Another task at about this level involves locating a particular intersection on a street map (249). One further task requires the reader to look at a paycheck stub summarizing wage information and directs the reader to write "gross pay for this year to date" in the

(Reduced from original copy.)

space provided (257). If the reader fails to match on both features — gross and year-to-date — he or she is likely to respond with an incorrect amount such as $625.00, or some other dollar amount.

Another question asked using this document was also expected to require a two-feature match — current and net pay — and therefore, to be approximately the same complexity. However, the analyses showed that this task was estimated to be about at the 200 level. Inspection of the paycheck stub reveals why this might be so. On this task the reader only has to match on a single feature because just one number is given in the column headed "net pay." Thus, the data suggest that this task is more like a one-feature match in terms of complexity and its estimated position on the document scale.

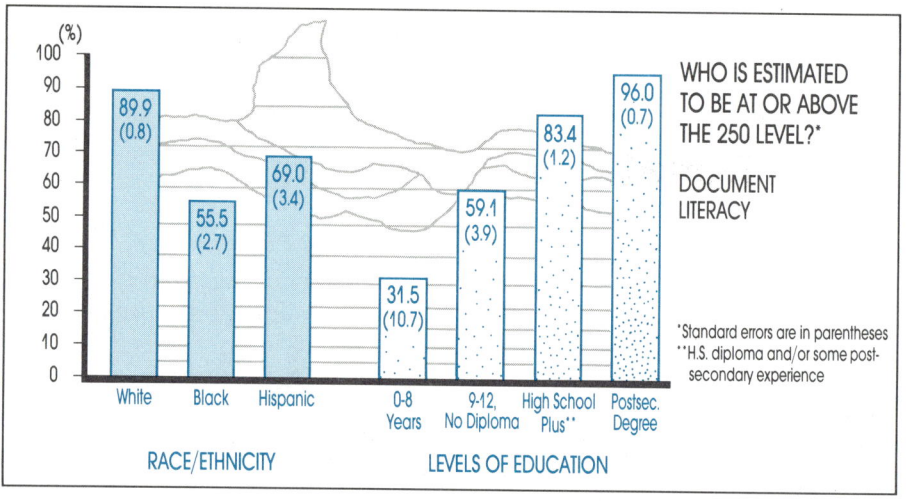

300 Level: 57% of Total Group

At this and higher levels of difficulty, the reader is asked to match information on the basis of increasing numbers of features. In some cases these are literal, while in others the matching is based on information that might be stated one way in the question and another in the document. Also common to these tasks is the increase in the number of distractors contained in the document. Examples of tasks having these characteristics are: identifying information contained in a graph depicting the source of energy, the year of consumption, and the percentage of use (294); and, looking up the appropriate kind of sandpaper to use from a chart depicting various types of use, grades, and materials to be sanded (320). Another type of task involves doing successive two-feature matching. This task requires the reader to follow directions using a street map to travel from one location to another (300).

The graph below shows predictions of United States energy consumption through the year 2000. Use the graph to answer the questions that follow.

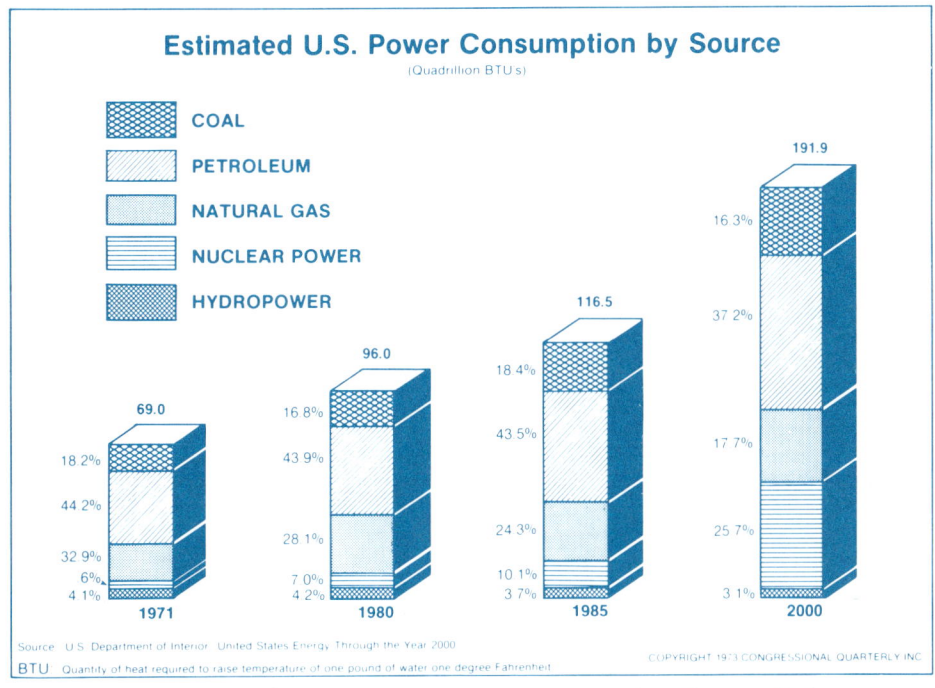

In the year 2000, which energy source is predicted to supply less power than coal?

A Petroleum
B Natural gas
C Nuclear power
D Hydropower
E I don't know.

(Reduced from original copy.)

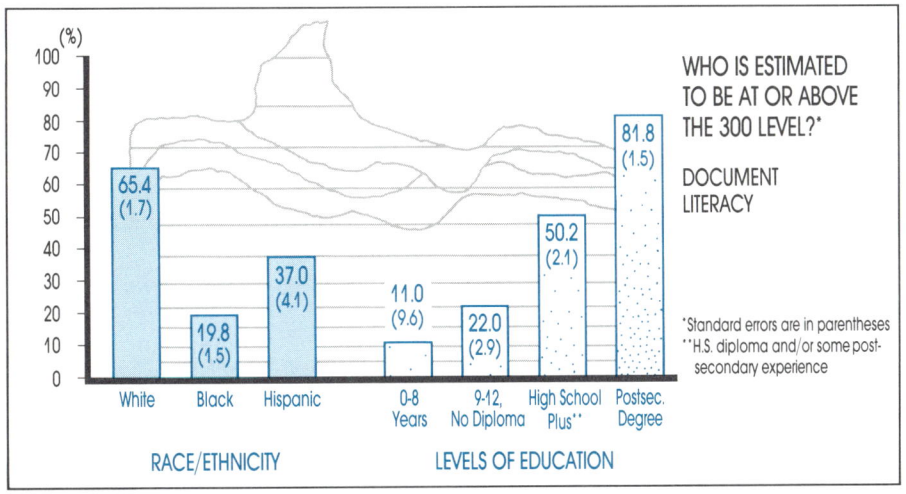

25

350 Level: 20% of Total Group

The most difficult task on this scale requires the reader to match on the basis of six features using a bus schedule (365) — Saturday, afternoon, missed the 2:35, leaving Hancock and Buena Ventura, arriving at Flintridge and Academy, how long is the wait for the next bus.

Refer to the following bus schedule for the Vista Grande route. Use the bus schedule to answer the questions.

ROUTE 5 — VISTA GRANDE

This bus line operates Monday through Saturday providing "local" service to most neighborhoods in the northeast section
Buses run thirty minutes apart during the morning and afternoon rush hours Monday through Friday
Buses run one hour apart at all other times of day and Saturday
No Sunday, holiday or night service.

OUTBOUND from Terminal

Leave Downtown Terminal	Leave Hancock and Buena Ventura	Leave Citadel	Leave Rustic Hills	Leave North Carefree and Oro Blanco	Arrive Flintridge and Academy
6:20	6:35	6:45	6:50	7:03	7:15
6:50	7:05	7:15	7:20	7:33	7:45
7:20	7:35	7:45	7:50	8:03	8:15
7:50	**8:05**	**8:15**	**8:20**	**8:33**	**8:45**
8:20	8:35	8:45	8:50	9:03	9:15
8:50	**9:05**	**9:15**	**9:20**	**9:33**	**9:45**
9:20	9:35	9:45	9:50	10:03	10:15
10:20	10:35	10:45	10:50	11:03	11:15
11:20	11:35	11:45	11:50	12:03	12:15
12:20	12:35	12:45	12:50	1:03	1:15
1:20	1:35	1:45	1:50	2:03	2:15
2:20	2:35	2:45	2:50	3:03	3:15
2:50	**3:05**	**3:15**	**3:20**	**3:33**	**3:45**
3:20	3:35	3:45	3:50	4:03	4:15
3:50	**4:05**	**4:15**	**4:20**	**4:33**	**4:45**
4:20	4:35	4:45	4:50	5:03	5:15
4:50	**5:05**	**5:15**	**5:20**	**5:33**	**5:45**
5:20	5:35	5:45	5:50	6:03	6:15
5:50	**6:05**	**6:15**	**6:20**	**6:33**	**6:45**
6:20	6:35	6:45	6:50	7:03	7:15

INBOUND toward Terminal

Leave Flintridge and Academy	Leave North Carefree and Oro Blanco	Leave Rustic Hills	Leave Citadel	Leave Hancock and Buena Ventura	Arrive Downtown Terminal
6:15	6:27	6:42	6:47	6:57	7:15
6:45	6:57	7:12	7:17	7:27	7:45 Monday through Friday only
7:15	7:27	7:42	7:47	7:57	8:15
7:45	7:57	8:12	8:17	8:27	8:45 Monday through Friday only
8:15	8:27	8:42	8:47	8:57	9:15
8:45	8:57	9:12	9:17	9:27	9:45 Monday through Friday only
9:15	9:27	9:42	9:47	9:57	10:15
9:45	9:57	10:12	10:17	10:27	10:45 Monday through Friday only
10:15	10:27	10:42	10:47	10:57	11:15
11:15	11:27	11:42	11:47	11:57	12:15
12:15	12:27	12:42 p.m.	12:47 p.m.	12:57 p.m.	1:15 p.m.
1:15	1:27	1:42	1:47	1:57	2:15
2:15	2:27	2:42	2:47	2:57	3:15
3:15	3:27	3:42	3:47	3:57	4:15
3:45	3:57	4:12	4:17	4:27	4:45 Monday through Friday only
4:15	4:27	4:42	4:47	4:57	5:15
4:45	4:57	5:12	5:17	5:27	5:45 Monday through Friday only
5:15	5:27	5:42	5:47	5:57	6:15
5:45	5:57	6:12	6:17	6:27	6:45 Monday through Friday only
					Monday through Friday only

You can transfer from this bus to another headed anywhere else in the city bus system.

To be sure of a smooth transfer tell the driver of this bus the name of the second bus you need.

On Saturday afternoon, if you miss the 2:35 bus leaving Hancock and Buena Ventura going to Flintridge and Academy, how long will you have to wait for the next bus?

   A Until 2:57 p.m.

   B Until 3:05 p.m.

   C Until 3:35 p.m.

   D Until 3:57 p.m.

   E I don't know.

(Reduced from original copy.)

Another task (334) using this same schedule requires the reader to match on fewer features and is below 350 on the scale. This task requires that the reader match on four features — Saturday, morning, second bus, arrive Downtown Terminal.

On Saturday morning, what time does the second bus arrive at the Downtown Terminal?

A 6:50 a.m.

B 7:45 a.m.

C 8:15 a.m.

D 8:45 a.m.

E I don't know.

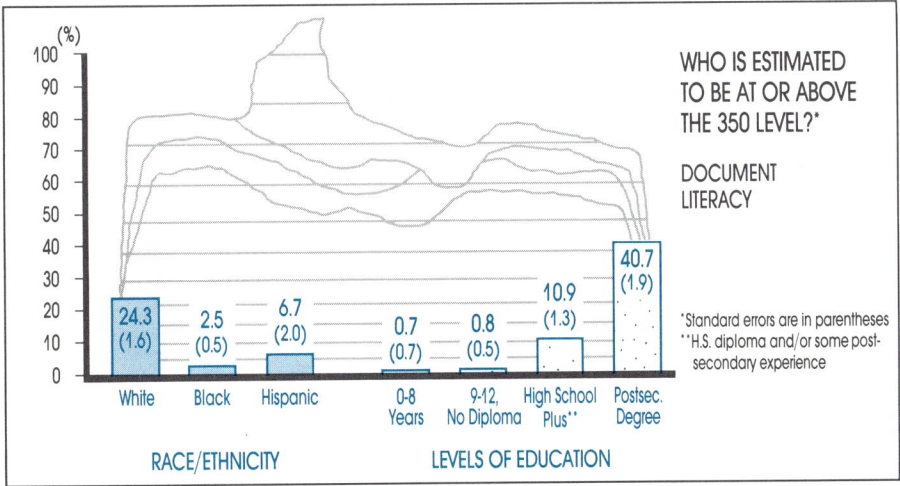

Summarizing Levels of Proficiency on the Document Scale. Table 3 summarizes performance on the document scale. Most young adults are estimated to perform at levels of proficiency associated with the least complex document tasks — up to the 175 level. This is true for all racial/ethnic groups and for all reported levels of education. The overwhelming majority are estimated to perform tasks characteristic of the 200 level, although 18 in 100 Black and eight in 100 Hispanic young adults are estimated to be below this level of proficiency.

The great majority of young adults are still performing at or above the 250 level, although there are some sharp drops for particular groups. For example, just over five in 10 Black young adults are estimated to have attained this level of proficiency compared with seven in 10 Hispanic and nine in 10 White young adults. In terms of educational experiences, just three in 10 young adults with 0 to 8 years of education

Percentages of People and Selected Tasks At or Above Successive Points on the Document Scale*

Selected Tasks at Decreasing Levels of Difficulty**	Selected Points on the Scale	Total
365 ⎫ Use bus schedule to select appropriate bus for given departures & arrivals	500	
343 ⎬	375	8.8 (0.8)
334 ⎭	350	20.2 (1.3)
320 Use sandpaper chart to locate appropriate grade given specifications	325	37.6 (1.6)
300 Follow directions to travel from one location to another using a map		
294 Identify information from graph depicting source of energy and year	300	57.2 (1.7)
278 Use index from an almanac		
262 Locate eligibility from table of employee benefits	275	73.1 (1.2)
257 Locate gross pay-to-date on pay stub		
255 Complete a check given information on a bill		
253 Complete an address on order form		
249 Locate intersection on street map	250	83.8 (1.0)
221 Enter date on a deposit slip	225	91.0 (0.8)
219 Identify cost of theatre trip from notice		
211 Match items on shopping list to coupons		
196 Enter personal information on job application	200	95.5 (0.5)
192 Locate movie in TV listing in newspaper		
181 Enter caller's number on phone message form		
169 Locate time of meeting on a form	175	98.4 (0.3)
160 Locate expiration date on driver's license		
110 Sign your name	150 / 0	99.7 (0.1)

**Number indicating difficulty level designates that point on the scale at which individuals with that level of proficiency have an 80 percent probability of responding correctly.

TABLE 3

Race/Ethnicity			Levels of Education			
White	Black	Hispanic	0-8 Years	9-12 Years	H.S. Diploma and/or More‡	2- or 4-Yr. Deg. or More
10.5 (1.0)	0.9 (0.4)	3.2 (1.6)	0.0 (0.0)	0.0 (0.0)	2.6 (0.5)	20.7 (1.4)
24.3 (1.6)	2.5 (0.5)	6.7 (2.0)	0.7 (0.7)	0.8 (0.5)	10.9 (1.3)	40.7 (1.9)
44.0 (1.8)	9.0 (1.1)	20.8 (3.1)	0.7 (0.7)	7.5 (1.4)	28.0 (1.7)	63.2 (1.8)
65.4 (1.7)	19.8 (1.5)	37.0 (4.1)	11.0 (9.6)	22.0 (2.9)	50.2 (2.1)	81.8 (1.5)
80.8 (1.1)	38.7 (2.6)	54.7 (3.8)	21.1 (12.4)	39.5 (3.6)	70.6 (1.5)	91.4 (1.0)
89.9 (0.8)	55.5 (2.7)	69.0 (3.4)	31.5 (10.7)	59.1 (3.9)	83.4 (1.2)	96.0 (0.7)
95.0 (0.7)	71.0 (2.2)	84.4 (1.6)	47.3 (9.5)	72.0 (3.3)	91.8 (0.8)	98.9 (0.3)
97.9 (0.5)	82.3 (1.7)	91.5 (1.2)	61.8 (7.7)	84.0 (2.7)	96.9 (0.5)	99.4 (0.2)
99.3 (0.3)	93.2 (1.2)	96.5 (0.7)	75.7 (6.3)	94.2 (1.2)	99.2 (0.2)	99.9 (0.0)
99.9 (0.1)	98.6 (0.4)	99.1 (0.3)	96.7 (2.7)	98.8 (0.3)	99.8 (0.1)	100.0 (0.0)

*Numbers in parentheses are estimated standard errors.
‡High school diploma and/or some postsecondary experience.

and six in 10 young adults with some high school experience are estimated to have attained this level. More than eight in 10 with a high school diploma and/or some postsecondary experience and almost all young adults who have earned a postsecondary degree are estimated to be at this level.

Although more than half (57.2 percent) of the young adults are still successful at or above the 300 level on the document scale, the contrasts among particular groups are telling. Compared with seven out of 10 White, just two in 10 Black and four in 10 Hispanic young adults achieve at or above this 300 level. More alarming is the fact that only one in 10 young adults with 0 to 8 years of education and two in 10 who have some high school experience are estimated to have mastered the skills and strategies associated with the 300 level on the document scale.

The 350 level is characterized by tasks requiring the most demanding information-processing skills and strategies assessed. Only 20 in 100 young adults are estimated to be performing at or above this 350 level. While only 25 in 100 White young adults attain this or higher levels on the document scale, just three in 100 Black and seven in 100 Hispanic young adults achieve these levels. Similarly, 40 in 100 young adults who earned postsecondary degrees achieve at these most challenging levels compared with 10 in 100 who have high school diplomas or some postsecondary experience. Less than one in 100 of those young adults not attaining high school diplomas is estimated to be at this or higher levels.

Quantitative Literacy

Successful performance on the quantitative scale requires the use of mathematical operations such as addition, subtraction, multiplication, and division — either singly or in combination — to solve problems that are embedded to varying degrees in printed material. Proficiency on this scale seems to be a function of the particular operation called for, the number of operations needed to perform the task, and the extent to which the numerical task is embedded in printed material. As a result, there is some overlap in the skills and strategies required on the quantitative scale with those needed on the prose and document literacy scales as evidenced by moderate correlations (.49 and .56, respectively).

225 Level: 92% of Total Group

The task that best typifies the lowest level on the quantitative scale requires totaling two entries on a bank deposit slip (233).

NATIONAL BANK			Dollars	Cents
		CASH	57	23
(Please Print)	Please use your personalized deposit tickets. If you need more, see your personal banker.	CHECKS List Singly	300	00
Name _____	BE SURE EACH ITEM IS PROPERLY ENDORSED			
_____ 19 ____				
	Total Items	TOTAL		

CHECKS AND OTHER ITEMS ARE RECEIVED FOR DEPOSIT SUBJECT TO THE PROVISIONS OF THE UNIFORM COMMERCIAL CODE OR ANY APPLICABLE COLLECTION AGREEMENT.

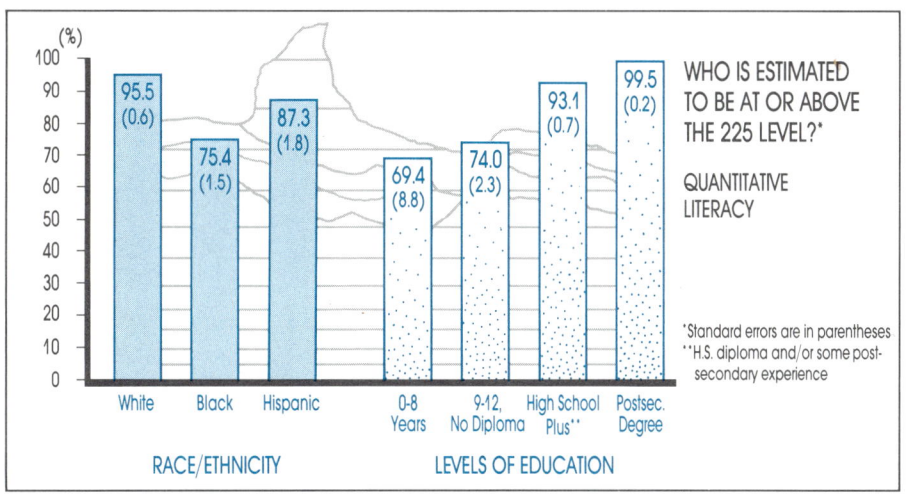

WHO IS ESTIMATED TO BE AT OR ABOVE THE 225 LEVEL?*

QUANTITATIVE LITERACY

*Standard errors are in parentheses
**H.S. diploma and/or some post-secondary experience

Race/Ethnicity: White 95.5 (0.6), Black 75.4 (1.5), Hispanic 87.3 (1.8)
Levels of Education: 0-8 Years 69.4 (8.8), 9-12, No Diploma 74.0 (2.3), High School Plus** 93.1 (0.7), Postsec. Degree 99.5 (0.2)

275 Level: 72% of Total Group

Tasks estimated to be slightly above the 275 level involve entering deposits and checks and balancing a checkbook. These range from 281 to 293.

Complete the check ledger for the month of September. Keep a running total of the balance and include the following:

$50 deposit on 9/27

check 108 payable to Mr. Davis for $18.49 on 9/27

check 109 payable to Electric Co. for $53 on 9/28

the $5 monthly service fee for your checking account

RECORD ALL CHARGES OR CREDITS THAT AFFECT YOUR ACCOUNT

NUMBER	DATE	DESCRIPTION OF TRANSACTION	PAYMENT/DEBT (−)	√T	FEE (IF ANY) (−)	DEPOSIT/CREDIT (+)	BALANCE
			$		$	$	$ 130 15
107	9/25	Martin's Grocery	24 76				105 39
	9/26	Paycheck				375 10	480 49

(Reduced from original copy.)

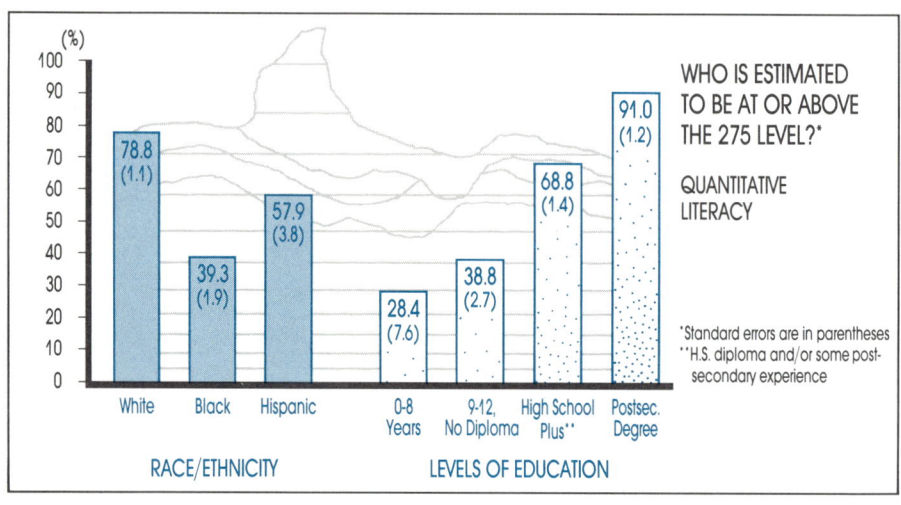

WHO IS ESTIMATED TO BE AT OR ABOVE THE 275 LEVEL?*

QUANTITATIVE LITERACY

*Standard errors are in parentheses
**H.S. diploma and/or some post-secondary experience

White 78.8 (1.1)
Black 39.3 (1.9)
Hispanic 57.9 (3.8)
0-8 Years 28.4 (7.6)
9-12, No Diploma 38.8 (2.7)
High School Plus** 68.8 (1.4)
Postsec. Degree 91.0 (1.2)

RACE/ETHNICITY   LEVELS OF EDUCATION

325 Level: 38% of Total Group

A task typical of performance at the 325 level requires the reader to examine a menu to compute the cost of a specified meal and to determine the correct change from a specified amount (337). The difficulty of such tasks reflects the need to match information and then to apply two operations in sequence.

Suppose you had $3.00 to spend for lunch.

If you order a Lancaster Special sandwich and onion soup, how much change would you get back? _____

How much should you leave for a 10% tip? _____

Soups — Made by our Chef Daily

Onion soup	.60
Soup of the day	.60
Vichyssoise in Summer	
Beef-burgers, broiled to order;	1.85
¼ lb. of the finest Beef available, seasoned to perfection and served on a buttered bun	
Wine Cheddar-cheese burger	1.95
Blue-cheese burger	1.95
Pineapple burger	1.95
Bacon burger	2.10
Wine Cheddar-cheese & Bacon burger	2.25

Sandwiches

Sliced Turkey — Garnished	1.30
Turkey Salad — Garnished	.95
Chicken Salad — Garnished	.95
Tuna Fish Salad — Garnished	.95
Sliced Beef Tongue — Garnished	1.50
Grilled Wine Cheddar-Cheese	.75
The Lancaster Special	1.95
Corned Beef, Melted Swiss Cheese, Sauerkraut on Seeded Rye . . . Need we say more?	

Minimum Check at Lunch 1.00

(Reduced from original copy.)

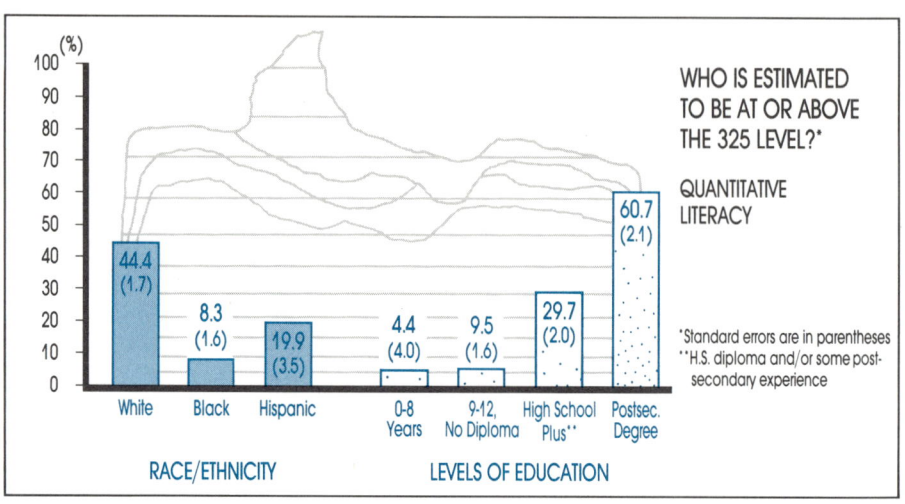

375 Level: 10% of Total Group

One task that typifies performance at the 375 level requires the reader to use a page from a catalogue to fill out an order form, calculate the costs for a number of items, and total the costs (371). Another task presents unit pricing information similar to that found in a grocery store; the reader is required to select the least costly product (376).

You need to buy peanut butter and are deciding between two brands.

Estimate the cost per ounce of the creamy peanut butter. Write your estimate on the line provided. _____

Circle the letter next to the more economical brand.

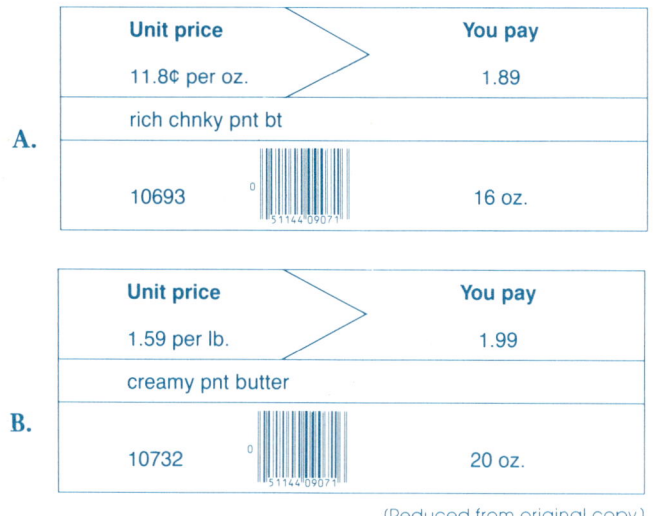

(Reduced from original copy.)

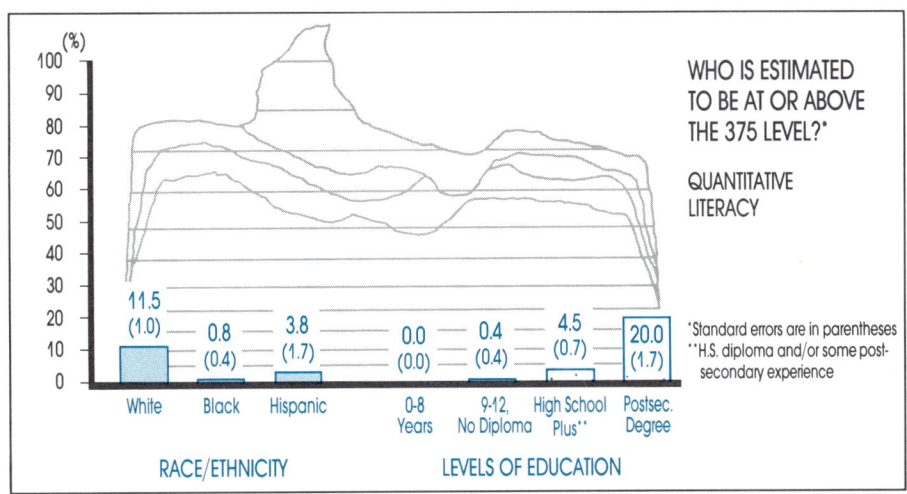

Summarizing Levels of Proficiency on the Quantitative Scale. Readers who successfully perform tasks on the quantitative scale apply arithmetic operations — addition, subtraction, multiplication, and division — as necessary to use printed materials encountered in everyday practical situations. Table 4 summarizes performance on the quantitative scale. The easiest task on the scale requires the reader to add two deposits that have already been entered on a bank deposit slip (233). The overwhelming majority of young adults are estimated to be at or above the 225 level and seven of 10 young adults with 0 to 8 years of education are estimated to be at or above this level.

Between the 275 and 300 levels, tasks not only require the performance of a single numeric operation such as addition or subtraction, but the accurate transfer of information onto a form (e.g., keeping a running balance in a checkbook). Seventy-two out of 100 young adults are estimated to be at or above the 275 level while 56 of 100 are estimated to be at or above the 300 level. As with the prose and document scales it is at about the 275 level that there is a sharp drop in the estimated proficiency of particular groups. For example, while roughly 91 of 100 young adults who have earned a postsecondary degree typically would be successful on tasks at this level, only about 28 in 100 young adults reporting up to eight years of schooling are estimated to be at or above the 275 level. Moreover, approximately 39 of 100 young adults reporting some high school experience and 69 of 100 earning high school diplomas or having some postsecondary school experience attain this or higher levels.

At higher levels on this scale (375), there are relatively few young adults from any group. For example, only about 12 in 100 White and 20 in 100 young adults with postsecondary degrees are estimated to be at or above this level. By comparison, only about one in 100 Black and four in 100 Hispanic young adults and only about five in 100 high school graduates attain this or higher levels.

Percentages of People and Selected Tasks At or Above Successive Points on the Quantitative Scale*

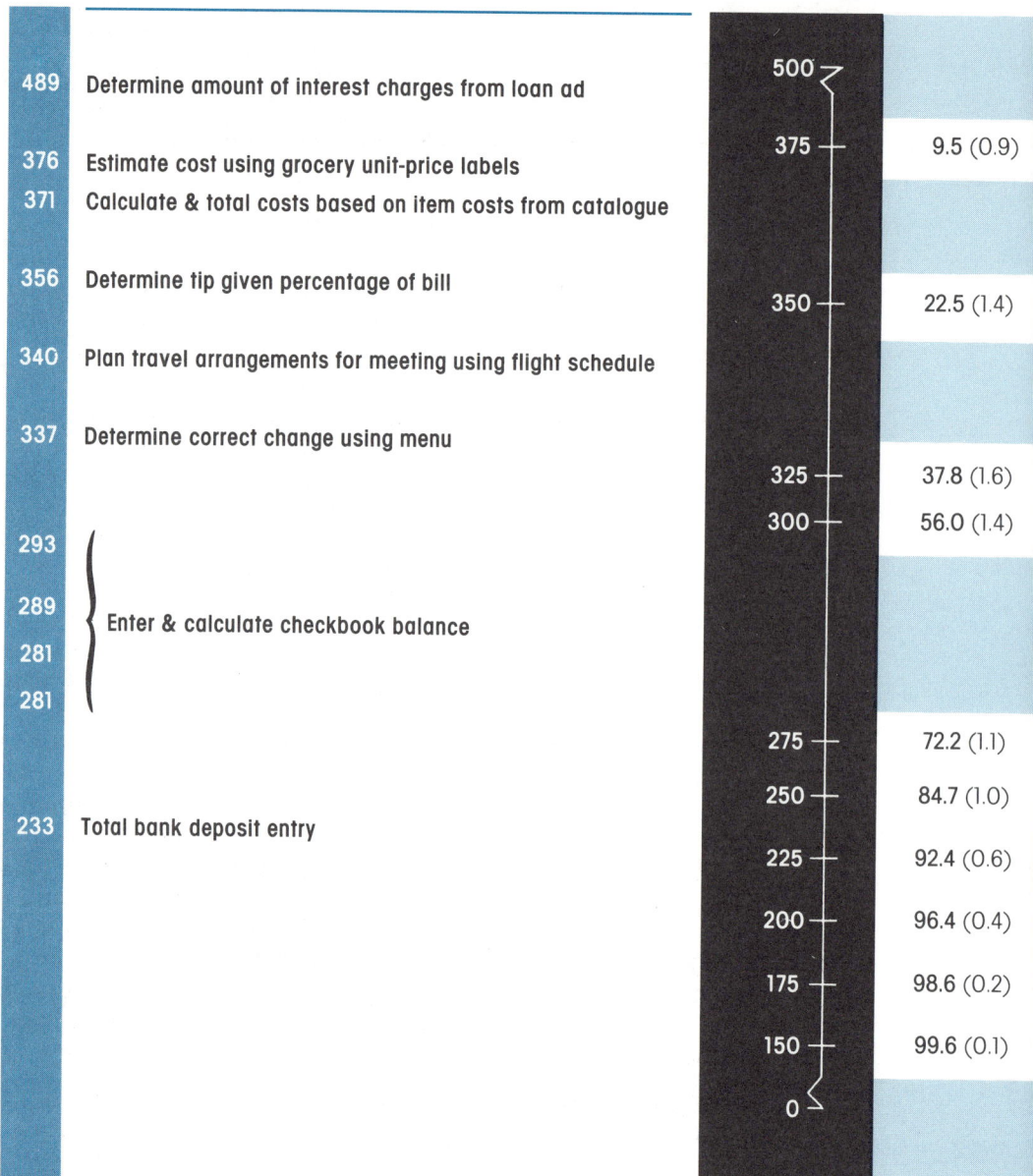

Selected Tasks at Decreasing Levels of Difficulty**	Selected Points on the Scale	Total
489 Determine amount of interest charges from loan ad	500	
376 Estimate cost using grocery unit-price labels	375	9.5 (0.9)
371 Calculate & total costs based on item costs from catalogue		
356 Determine tip given percentage of bill	350	22.5 (1.4)
340 Plan travel arrangements for meeting using flight schedule		
337 Determine correct change using menu		
	325	37.8 (1.6)
	300	56.0 (1.4)
293 ⎫		
289 ⎬ Enter & calculate checkbook balance		
281 ⎪		
281 ⎭		
	275	72.2 (1.1)
	250	84.7 (1.0)
233 Total bank deposit entry		
	225	92.4 (0.6)
	200	96.4 (0.4)
	175	98.6 (0.2)
	150	99.6 (0.1)
	0	

**Number indicating difficulty level designates that point on the scale at which individuals with that level of proficiency have an 80 percent probability of responding correctly.

TABLE 4

Race/Ethnicity			Levels of Education			
White	Black	Hispanic	0-8 Years	9-12 Years	H.S. Diploma and/or More‡	2- or 4-Yr. Deg. or More
11.5 (1.0)	0.8 (0.4)	3.8 (1.7)	0.0 (0.0)	0.4 (0.4)	4.5 (0.7)	20.0 (1.7)
27.2 (1.7)	2.4 (0.8)	11.3 (2.7)	4.4 (4.0)	2.3 (0.8)	13.4 (1.3)	42.9 (2.3)
44.4 (1.7)	8.3 (1.6)	19.9 (3.5)	4.4 (4.0)	9.5 (1.6)	29.7 (2.0)	60.7 (2.1)
63.3 (1.5)	22.0 (2.1)	36.9 (4.4)	8.5 (4.5)	20.9 (2.7)	49.4 (1.9)	79.8 (1.6)
78.8 (1.1)	39.3 (1.9)	57.9 (3.8)	28.4 (7.6)	38.8 (2.7)	68.8 (1.4)	91.0 (1.2)
89.4 (0.9)	60.4 (2.5)	74.6 (3.0)	48.2 (12.3)	61.5 (3.2)	83.0 (1.1)	97.4 (0.7)
95.5 (0.6)	75.4 (1.5)	87.3 (1.8)	69.4 (8.8)	74.0 (2.3)	93.1 (0.7)	99.5 (0.2)
98.0 (0.4)	87.4 (1.5)	93.1 (1.3)	81.5 (5.9)	85.9 (2.0)	97.2 (0.5)	99.8 (0.1)
99.2 (0.2)	94.8 (0.9)	97.7 (0.6)	91.5 (2.9)	94.3 (1.2)	99.0 (0.2)	99.9 (0.0)
99.8 (0.1)	98.3 (0.5)	99.6 (0.3)	96.0 (2.1)	98.3 (0.6)	99.9 (0.1)	100.0 (0.0)

*Numbers in parentheses are estimated standard errors.
‡High school diploma and/or some postsecondary experience.

Section 2
Comparing Young Adults With NAEP's In-School Population

The *Reading Report Card** reported the proficiencies of in-school 9-, 13-, and 17-year-olds based on a nationally representative sample of some 70,000 students. With few exceptions, the exercises included in the 1983-84 reading assessment were multiple-choice and similar in content and length to traditional tests of reading achievement.

To enhance the interpretability of results, reading exercises administered across the three ages were placed on a common scale ranging from 0 to 500 with an average of 250 and a standard deviation of 50. The estimated average reading proficiencies for NAEP's in-school population of 9-, 13-, and 17-year-olds are 213.2, 257.8, and 288.2, respectively.

A major goal of the current study was to link the performance of young adults to that of students participating in the NAEP reading assessment of 1983-84. To accomplish this goal, a representative set of exercises from the NAEP reading scale was added to the young adult literacy assessment to allow estimates of the performance of young adults on the NAEP reading scale.

To aid in the interpretation of the reading scale, NAEP identified and described performance at each of five levels reproduced below.

Rudimentary (150): Performance at this level suggests the ability to carry out simple, discrete reading tasks.

Basic (200): Performance at this level suggests the ability to understand specific or sequentially related information.

Intermediate (250): Performance at this level suggests the ability to search for specific information, interrelate ideas, and make generalizations.

**The Reading Report Card: Progress Toward Excellence in Our Schools, Trends in Reading Over Four National Assessments, 1971-1984.* Princeton. N.J.: National Assessment of Educational Progress, Report 15-R-01, 1985.

Adept (300): Performance at this level suggests the ability to find, understand, summarize, and explain relatively complicated information.

Advanced (350): Performance at this level suggests the ability to synthesize and learn from specialized reading materials.

Differences would be expected between the performances of young adults and in-school 17-year-old students. On the one hand, the NAEP sample does not include 17-year-olds who dropped out of school, and so one would expect the NAEP 1983-84 results to overestimate somewhat the reading proficiency of all 17-year-olds. On the other hand, one would also expect that reading skills would increase with use in practical situations after the termination of formal education or during the pursuit of higher education.

Young Adults and In-School 17-Year-Olds

The performance of young adults compared to that of the in-school 17-year-olds shown in Table 5 are remarkably similar at each of the lower three levels of reading comprehension — Rudimentary, Basic, and Intermediate. However, it is important to recognize that there is a

TABLE 5

Comparisons of Percentages of Young Adults with In-School 17-Year-Olds At or Above Each of the Five Levels of Proficiency on the NAEP Reading Scale for Total and Racial/Ethnic Groups*

	Advanced 350	Adept 300	Intermediate 250	Basic 200	Rudimentary 150
Total					
Young Adults	20.9 (1.4)	54.4 (1.6)	84.1 (0.7)	96.8 (0.4)	99.6 (0.2)
17-Year Olds	4.9 (0.2)	39.2 (0.8)	83.6 (0.7)	98.6 (0.1)	100.0 (0.0)
Ethnicity/Race					
White					
Young Adults	24.5 (1.6)	60.7 (1.6)	88.7 (0.6)	98.2 (0.5)	99.7 (0.1)
17-Year Olds	5.8 (0.2)	45.1 (0.8)	88.9 (0.5)	99.2 (0.1)	100.0 (0.0)
Black					
Young Adults	3.9 (0.9)	24.9 (2.4)	61.1 (2.0)	89.9 (1.2)	98.8 (0.4)
17-Year Olds	0.8 (0.2)	15.5 (1.0)	65.8 (1.2)	96.5 (0.3)	100.0 (0.0)
Hispanic					
Young Adults	9.5 (1.7)	40.6 (2.9)	76.0 (2.7)	95.9 (1.0)	99.5 (0.4)
17-Year Olds	1.5 (0.3)**	19.9 (1.8)**	69.1 (1.7)**	96.8 (0.4)**	100.0 (0.0)**

*Numbers in parentheses are estimated standard errors.
**These standard errors could not be estimated precisely.

striking increase in the percentage of young adults achieving at the two highest levels of reading comprehension (Adept and Advanced) as compared with the in-school 17-year-olds. For the total young adult population, 54 in 100 attain the 300 or Adept level as compared with 39 in 100 of the 17-year-olds. At the Advanced level, the difference in proficiency is even more pronounced — more than four times as many young adults as 17-year-olds (proportionally) are estimated to have advanced reading skills. This pattern is relatively consistent across each of the three racial/ethnic groups, but it should be noted that fewer Black young adults than Black 17-year-old students attain the Basic and Intermediate levels. The fact that young adults, on average, surpass the performance of in-school 17-year-olds — 54 of 100 young adults reach or surpass the 300 level as compared with 39 of 100 in-school 17-year-olds — probably reflects a combination of continued participation in formal education and participation in society.

Comparing Young Adults to Three Grade Levels

While it is useful to compare young adults with the performance of in-school 17-year-olds, typical comparisons in our society are based on the average performance of students at particular grade levels. For the 1983-84 assessment, NAEP data were collected not only by age but by grade level as well (grades 4, 8, and 11). Table 6 gives the estimated percent of young adults (total group, level of education, and by race/ethnicity) in relation to the average reading proficiency scores of fourth, eighth, and eleventh graders.

It is of course reassuring to note that about 94 out of 100 young adults read at or above the level of the average fourth grader and roughly 80 out of 100 in this total population reach or exceed the eighth grade level of average proficiency. Perhaps most interesting is the fact that around 62 in 100 young adults read as well as or better than the typical eleventh grader. These results reinforce the conclusion that "illiteracy" is not a *major* problem for this population.

Percentages of Young Adult Populations At or Above Average Reading Proficiency of 4th, 8th, and 11th Graders on the NAEP Scale*

TABLE 6

NAEP Average Reading Proficiencies at 3 Grade Levels		Total	Level of Education				Race/Ethnicity		
			0-8 yrs.	9-12, No Diploma	H.S. Diploma and/or More	Postsecondary Degree	White	Black	Hispanic
Grade 11	289.3 (0.8)	61.5	15.1	27.4	55.9	83.3	67.6	31.0	52.3
Grade 8	260.7 (0.5)	79.8	37.0	53.6	77.9	95.6	85.0	53.0	70.9
Grade 4	217.5 (0.7)	94.0	73.3	76.1	94.7	99.6	96.2	82.2	92.4

*The percents given in this table were estimated based on average NAEP scores at or above 218, 260 and 290. These are rounded from means shown in column 1 of the table.

The news is not all good, however. While the differences in performance between males and females are trivial, those between the racial/ethnic groups and levels of educational attainment are of concern. For example, more than 96 out of 100 White young adults are estimated to read at or above the level of the average fourth grader; however, roughly 92 out of 100 Hispanic, and only about 82 of 100 Black young adults are estimated to have attained or exceeded this roughly Basic level. At about the level of the average eighth grader, there are 85 in 100 White young adults as compared with 71 in 100 Hispanic and only 53 in 100 Black young adults. By grade 11, the numbers for White, Hispanic, and Black young adults drop to approximately 68 in 100, 52 in 100, and 31 in 100, respectively. Nevertheless, there is evidence from NAEP in-school assessments *(The Reading Report Card)* that the reading proficiencies of minority students are increasing at a faster rate than those of their White majority peers.

The relationship between education and reading achievement is also revealed in Table 6 by the percentages of young adults who have attained various levels of education. For example, while 76 in 100 young adults with some high school experience reach or surpass the reading level of the average fourth grader, roughly 54 of 100 and 27 of 100 reach or surpass the average eighth or eleventh grader, respectively. In contrast, for those young adults who have earned postsecondary school degrees, virtually all reach or surpass the performance of the average fourth grader, and approximately 96 of 100 and 83 of 100 reach or surpass the average performance of eighth and eleventh graders, respectively.

While we typically make comparisons of reading achievement on the basis of average performance for students at particular grade levels, caution must be exercised in comparing the performance of adults to that of in-school students. This caution stems from two concerns. One, literacy goes beyond traditional measures of reading comprehension to include information-processing skills and strategies associated with a broad range of tasks not usually represented on typical standardized tests of reading achievement. This fact is in part demonstrated by the moderate degree of association found between performance on the NAEP scale and performance on the prose, document, and quantitative scales (the correlations are .58, .61, and .58, respectively).

Second, grade-level results represent the average performance of students functioning within a particular school context and, thus, reflect much more than simply reading achievement. Interpretation of performance should be quite different: Just as a fourth grader scoring at an eleventh-grade level on a test of reading achievement is very different from a tenth- or eleventh-grade student scoring at this level, so is an adult scoring at an eighth-grade level very different from a seventh or eighth grader demonstrating this level of reading achievement.

Section 3

Characterizing the Young Adults

A considerable amount of data were collected during the 30-minute background interview to provide not only personal information characteristic of the 21- to 25-year-olds in this country but also information that might be related to differences in literacy skills among young adults. This section describes young adults in terms of:

- Age at which English was learned
- Access to literacy materials in the home
- Parents' levels of education
- Young adults' levels of education
- Reasons reported for dropping out of school
- Studying for and completing the GED
- Current school enrollment
- Occupational status
- Current literacy activities

Age at Which English Was Learned

An important characteristic bearing on literacy skills is the influence of a language other than English spoken in the home. As shown in Table 7 roughly 15 percent of the total young adult population are estimated to have grown up in households where a language other than English was spoken. Among racial/ethnic groups, nearly 80 percent of Hispanic, 10 percent of White, and five percent of Black young adults are estimated to have come from such homes. The predominant speakers of a non-English language were the parents of the respondents. Of particular interest is the fact that only about 30 percent of these young adults reported "usually speaking" this non-English language while growing up (the percentages varied from 16 percent for White to 36 percent for Hispanic, to 42 percent for Black young adults). Among other things, the data in Table 7 show that simply reporting that a language other than English was spoken in the home is insufficient information from which to judge the predominant language spoken by the respondent.

For those respondents who themselves spoke a non-English language, the age at which they reported learning to speak English is of interest. Roughly 70 percent of Black and White young adults who spoke a non-English language learned to speak English before the age of five. In contrast, only about 40 percent of Hispanic young adults reported learning to speak English by the age of five, while nearly 80 percent said they had learned English by the age of 10. There seems to be an interesting relationship between age of learning English and parental education — significantly more of the young adults who learned to speak English before the age of five had parents who had attained some postsecondary education compared with those whose parents who did not complete high school.

TABLE 7
Percentages of Persons in the Household Usually Speaking a Language Other than English in the Home*

	Subtotal	Racial/Ethnic Group		
		White	Black	Hispanic
Father	70.4 (4.4)	61.5 (7.3)	73.2 (15.1)	76.9 (5.6)
Mother	79.3 (2.8)	70.5 (5.2)	72.2 (14.6)	88.0 (2.5)
Sibling	40.8 (3.4)	16.4 (3.0)	62.5 (21.8)	57.9 (4.5)
Relative	46.0 (3.2)	40.6 (4.1)	60.3 (16.6)	45.0 (5.9)
Non-Relative	16.7 (1.7)	10.7 (2.3)	20.0 (8.6)	21.1 (3.5)
Respondent	29.5 (3.1)	15.9 (3.8)	42.3 (7.4)	36.4 (4.2)
N	663	201	46	320
Weighted N	3,167,650	1,525,186	138,671	983,115
Percent of Total	15.3	9.5	5.2	77.7

*Numbers in parentheses are estimated standard errors.

Access to Literacy Materials in the Home

An additional characteristic of the home environment that traditionally relates to levels of proficiency is access to literacy materials in the home. Young adults were asked which of the following six types of materials were available in their homes while they were in high school:

- a daily or weekly newspaper
- magazines
- more than 25 books
- an encyclopedia
- a dictionary
- a personal computer

A "literacy materials" variable was developed by adding the number of "yes" responses to each of these six types. While there is a tendency for the education levels of respondents and their parents to be related to literacy materials in the home, none of the differences is statistically significant. Furthermore, there are no significant differences among Black, White, and Hispanic young adults suggesting that, on average, these groups had roughly equal access to a common set of basic literacy materials.

Levels of Parental Education

Parents' level of education relates to the early experiences of the respondents by functioning as an indicator (along with literacy materials in the home) of home educational support. From this perspective, parents have a strong influence on the educational aspirations and attainments of their children.

Figure 1 shows the relationship between reported levels of parental education and racial/ethnic group membership. On average, White young adults come from homes in which parents attain higher levels of education than either their Black or Hispanic peers. In fact, at the lowest level of education (0 to 8 years), Hispanic young adults are represented disproportionately — some 20 percent of Hispanic young adults have parents who received eight or fewer years of schooling as compared with approximately 10 percent and three percent for Black and White young adults, respectively.

Figure 1

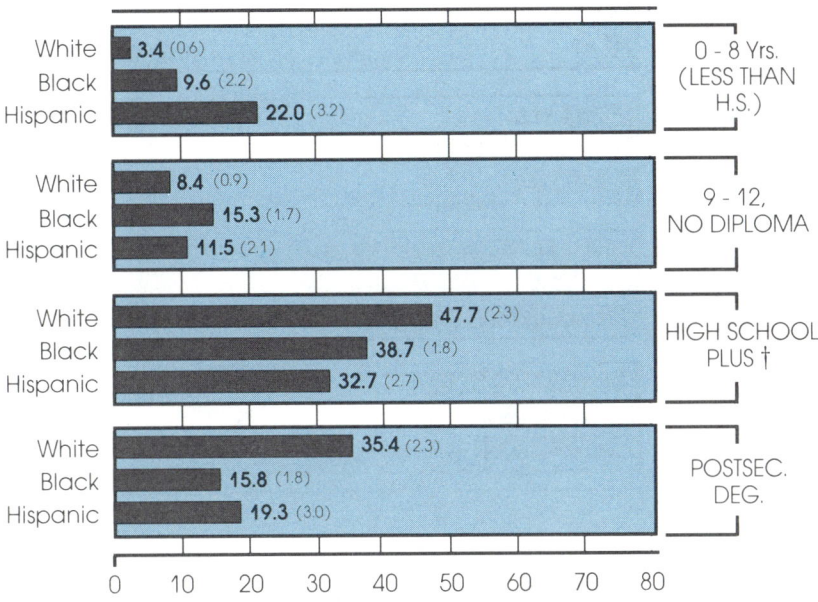

* Numbers in parentheses are estimated standard errors.
† High school diploma and/or some postsecondary experience.

Young Adults' Levels of Education

Similar to the information about parental education, on average, White young adults attain higher levels of education than do either Black or Hispanic young adults. Figure 2A shows that postsecondary degrees were received by nearly twice as many White young adults (40 percent) as by Black or Hispanic young adults (21 and 25 percent, respectively). On the other hand, nearly twice as many Black and Hispanic young adults (roughly 25 percent) terminated their formal education before receiving a high school diploma than did White young adults (about 13 percent). Moreover, more than twice as many Hispanic young adults (almost five percent) terminated their schooling with eight or fewer years as compared with Black and White young adults (nearly two percent).

As shown in Figure 2B, level of parental education is positively related to the education attained by young adults — that is, the higher the education level of parents, the higher the education level of young adults. It is interesting to note that young adults whose parents left school before receiving a high school diploma tend to complete more formal schooling than their parents.

45

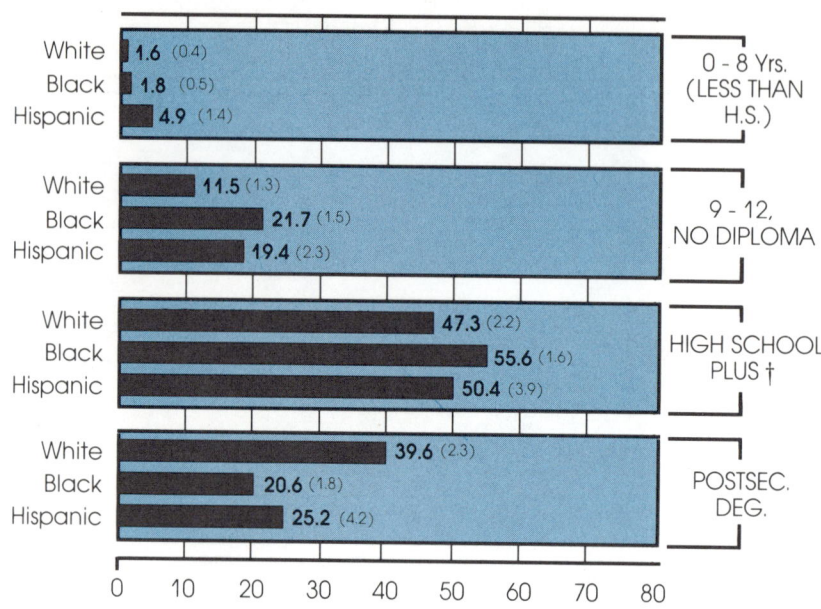

Figure 2A

YOUNG ADULTS' LEVELS OF EDUCATION
BY RACE/ETHNICITY*

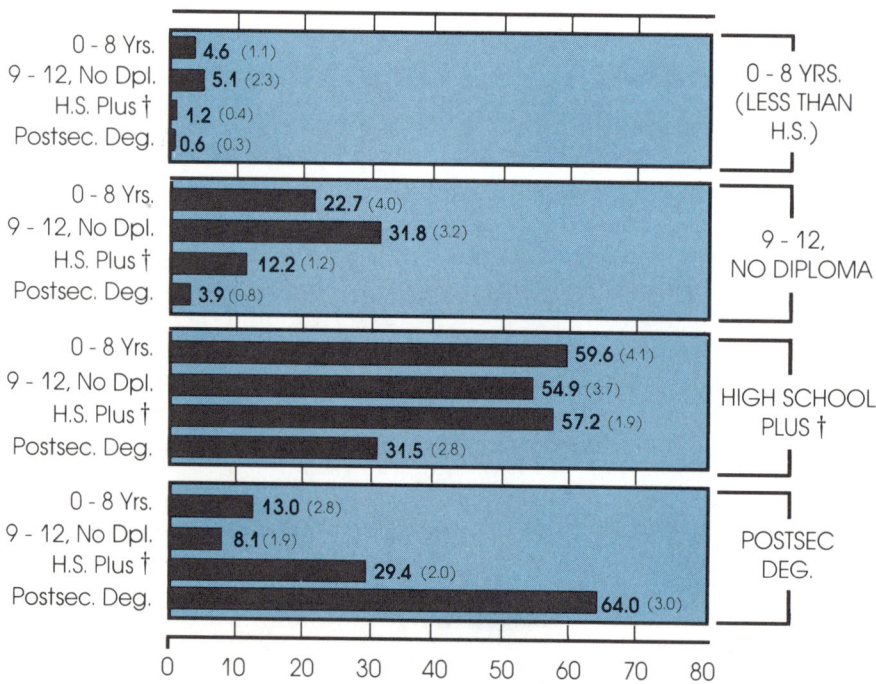

Figure 2B

BY LEVELS OF PARENTAL EDUCATION*

* Numbers in parentheses are estimated standard errors.
† High school diploma and/or some postsecondary experience.

Reported Reasons for Dropping Out of High School

While the question of educational attainment is important, it is also of interest to explore the reasons young adults give for not completing their high school education (Table 8). For Black young adults, the major reasons given are pregnancy and loss of interest in school. For White and Hispanic young adults the major reasons appear to be loss of interest and personal (relocation or marriage). Roughly 18 percent of White, Black, and Hispanic dropouts report leaving school to go to work or into the military. Surprisingly, relatively few respondents reported dropping out of school because of poor grades. This finding is in contrast to other studies* which indicate that poor academic performance is among the best predictors of school dropouts. These data most probably reflect the fact that, while academic performance is important in the decision to stay in or drop out of school, young adults *attribute* this decision to factors other than their academic performance.

*D. Rock, R. Ekstrom, M. Goertz, and J. Pollack, *Study of Excellence in High School Education, Longitudinal Study 1980-82, Final Report.* Princeton, N.J.: Educational Testing Service, 1985.

Reasons Given for Not Completing High School by Race/Ethnicity*

TABLE 8

	Race/Ethnicity			
	White	Black	Hispanic	Subtotal
Finance	2.1 (0.8)	1.7 (0.9)	4.4 (2.4)	2.5 (0.9)
Work	18.5 (2.7)	17.1 (3.3)	19.7 (3.8)	18.4 (1.8)
Pregnant	6.5 (1.5)	27.5 (6.5)	12.4 (4.9)	11.2 (2.0)
Boredom	39.3 (3.9)	30.4 (5.2)	26.3 (4.5)	36.5 (2.9)
Grades	3.3 (1.2)	3.4 (0.8)	4.5 (2.0)	3.3 (0.9)
Personal	29.5 (3.6)	17.7 (2.0)	32.1 (6.6)	27.1 (2.4)
N	300	249	114	679
Weighted N	2,047,289	626,895	304,499	3,078,748
Percent of Total	12.8	23.3	24.1	14.9

*Numbers in parentheses are estimated standard errors.

Young Adults Who Studied for and Completed the GED

Approximately half of the young adults who did not complete high school reported that they had studied for a GED. Figure 3A shows that this rate of GED program participation is relatively consistent regardless of racial/ethnic group membership. Although race/ethnicity does not seem to be related to participation in GED programs, respondents' elementary and secondary school experience and their parents' education levels are so related. While only one in three young adults who completed eight or fewer years of schooling reported studying for a GED, approximately one in two young adults who had some high school experience reported participation in a GED program. Moreover, significantly more young adults whose parents have postsecondary degrees reported participation in GED programs.

Probably of more concern than the question of who enrolls in a GED program is the question of who completes such programs. Figure 3B shows that neither previous school experience of the respondent nor parental education seems to be related to whether or not young adults complete the GED program, despite the fact that each was related to program participation. On the other hand, while racial/ethnic group membership is not significantly related to enrolling in a GED program, it is related to completion of a GED. Figure 3B shows that about four in 10 White and Hispanic young adults who study for a GED complete it, compared with only about two in 10 Black young adults.

Current Educational Status

One area of interest associated with the current activities of young adults involved their educational status at the time of this literacy assessment. Roughly one in four young adults reported being enrolled in school. Racial/ethnic group membership appears to have little relationship with enrollment status (Table 9). In contrast, both the level of parental education and the respondent's reported education level are related to current enrollment in school.

For example, with respect to parental education, more than three times as many young adults whose parents have postsecondary degrees (41 percent) were enrolled in school at the time of this assessment than those whose parents have some high school experience (12 percent). Falling between these two groups are young adults whose parents have graduated from high school and/or had some postsecondary experience (22 percent).

Table 9 indicates that education level is related not only to whether or not young adults are currently enrolled in school, but also to whether or not their enrollment is on a full-time or part-time basis.

Figure 3A

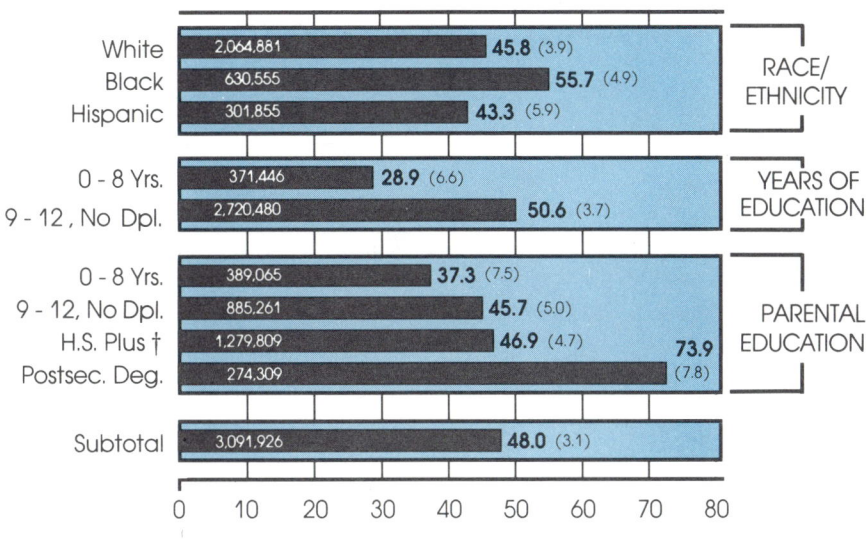

Figure 3B

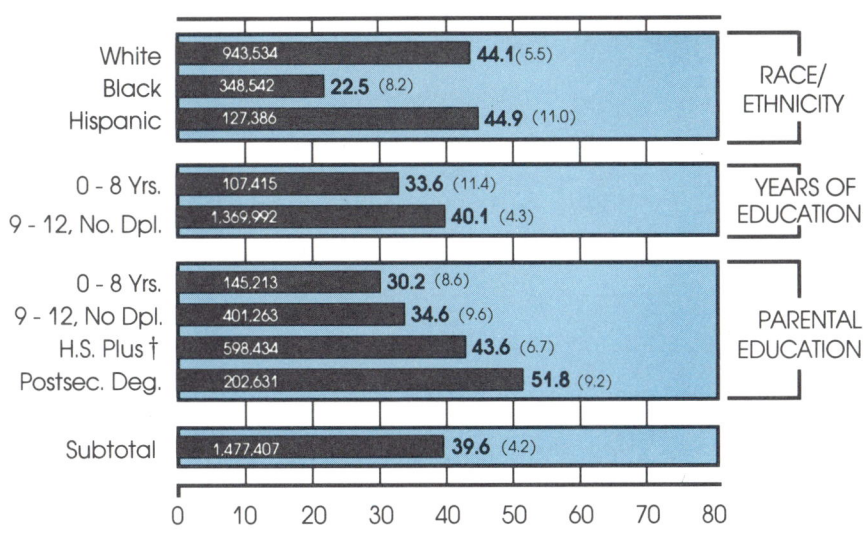

* Numbers in parentheses are estimated standard errors.
** Numbers in bars are weighted Ns.
† High school diploma and/or some postsecondary experience.

TABLE 9

Distributions of Young Adults Who Report Enrollment in School by Race/Ethnicity, Educational Attainment, and Parental Education*

	Population Currently Enrolled in School				
	N	Weighted N	Percent of Total	Full-time	Part-time
Race/Ethnicity					
White	535	4,172,390	26.5	68.7 (3.8)	31.3 (3.8)
Black	181	526,669	20.8	66.7 (5.2)	33.3 (5.2)
Hispanic	85	286,353	22.8	51.3 (8.0)	48.7 (8.0)
Educational Attainment					
Less than high school	3	54,467	14.5	9.3 (20.4)	90.7 (20.4)
Some high school	52	223,842	8.1	31.8 (10.4)	68.2 (10.4)
High school graduate and/or some postsecondary	305	1,680,323	17.2	52.3 (5.2)	47.7 (5.2)
Postsecondary degree	499	3,355,832	45.3	80.5 (3.1)	19.5 (3.1)
Parental Education					
Less than high school	54	195,669	14.9	59.5 (11.2)	40.5 (11.2)
Some high school	61	239,858	11.9	39.1 (11.5)	60.9 (11.5)
High school graduate and/or some postsecondary	351	2,108,742	22.4	62.6 (4.3)	37.4 (4.3)
Postsecondary degree	383	2,737,101	41.3	76.9 (4.0)	23.1 (4.0)
Subtotal	859	5,314,464	26.2	68.8 (3.7)	31.2 (3.7)

*Numbers in parentheses are estimated standard errors.

Almost four in 10 respondents whose parents had some high school experience were enrolled in school as full-time students. This number increases to six in 10 for those young adults whose parents graduated from high school and/or had some postsecondary school experience, and reaches almost eight in 10 for those whose parents had postsecondary degrees.

Young Adults' Occupational Status

Occupational status is also of interest for this young adult population but is confounded by the fact that so many people in this age range are still involved in the educational process. Nevertheless, it is still illuminating to look at the numbers of young adults who were and were not employed during the 12 months preceding this assessment.

It is readily seen in Table 10 that White young adults have the highest percentage of employment (88 percent) followed closely by both Hispanic (85 percent) and Black young adults (80 percent). However, it is also important to look at the activity of those young adults who were not employed — unemployed, in school, and keeping house. Approximately three times as many Black as White and almost twice as many Hispanic as White young adults report being unemployed during this period, with Black unemployment surpassing Hispanic unemployment by a three-to-two margin. Even more telling than racial/ethnic group membership is the expected relationship between the respondent's level of education and unemployment. Roughly 26 percent of those with 0 to 8 years of education reported being unemployed as compared with 22 percent for those with some high school, 15 percent for those with high school diplomas and/or some postsecondary experience, and only 4 percent for those with postsecondary degrees. There is a strikingly similar pattern of unemployment for level of parental education.

TABLE 10

Reported Employment Status of Young Adults by Race/Ethnicity, Educational Attainment, and Parental Education*

	Employed in Past 12 Months			Not Employed					
	N	Weighted N	Percent Saying Yes	N	Weighted N	Percent of Total	Unemployed	In School	Keeping House
Race/Ethnicity									
White	1,997	16,018,109	88.0 (1.0)	263	1,910,403	11.9	10.4 (2.4)	27.0 (4.1)	57.2 (4.5)
Black	957	2,693,192	79.5 (2.0)	242	546,310	20.3	30.0 (3.9)	25.9 (3.8)	38.1 (3.2)
Hispanic	391	1,264,984	84.6 (1.8)	76	193,114	15.3	18.4 (4.4)	18.7 (5.4)	59.5 (5.9)
Educational Attainment									
Less than high school	77	374,926	67.2 (6.9)	35	122,821	32.8	26.4 (9.8)	0.0 (0.0)	71.1 (10.0)
Some high school	618	2,769,840	74.2 (2.8)	201	704,299	25.4	21.6 (4.4)	5.0 (1.7)	67.7 (4.4)
High school graduate and/or some postsecondary	1,718	9,999,954	86.7 (1.2)	270	1,324,141	13.2	14.6 (3.0)	19.9 (4.3)	59.2 (4.6)
Postsecondary degree	1,058	7,565,453	90.9 (1.3)	109	683,598	9.0	3.6 (2.0)	81.0 (5.8)	12.4 (4.9)
Parental Education									
Less than high school	357	1,424,884	79.0 (3.2)	85	296,778	22.5	29.4 (7.1)	19.4 (6.1)	46.9 (8.6)
Some high school	489	2,400,960	78.4 (2.7)	131	518,619	25.7	21.3 (3.9)	10.1 (3.9)	66.2 (5.2)
High school graduate and/or some postsecondary	1,535	9,734,079	87.6 (1.3)	249	1,194,682	12.7	12.9 (2.9)	24.6 (5.0)	56.4 (4.3)
Postsecondary degree	978	6,737,472	89.2 (1.3)	115	728,219	11.0	3.0 (1.5)	60.0 (7.0)	31.6 (6.2)
Total	3,474	20,720,464	86.2 (0.9)	615	2,834,859	13.7	14.2 (2.0)	30.0 (4.3)	50.5 (3.8)

*Numbers in parentheses are estimated standard errors.

Current Literacy Activities

Despite the fact that large differences in literacy proficiency are found among various groups, an important issue for this assessment was to look at the literacy activities of these young adults. Information was gathered about contents within newspapers, and different magazines, books, and brief documents read.

- For newspapers, questions were asked about 13 content areas, including national/international and local news, comics, advertisements, sports, women's pages, financial news, book and movie reviews, and horoscopes.
- For magazines, young adults were asked to list up to five different magazines they read on a regular basis for work and up to five for their own enjoyment.
- With books, young adults were asked to indicate which of several types they read or used that included: fiction, history, science, recreation, entertainment, religion, references, and manuals.
- Brief documents included a list of 18 materials such as labels and tags, diagrams, tables, memos and notices, reports, and computer programs.

The overwhelming majority (at least 85 percent) of young adults report reading a newspaper and/or a magazine on a regular basis, reading and/or using a book within the last six months, and using brief documents. Table 11 provides a summary of the average number of content areas read within each of the four categories. Of particular interest is the fact that there are no differences among White, Black, and Hispanic young adults with respect to the average number of content areas in newspapers, and the average number of different books, magazines, or brief documents read. Even more surprising is that neither respondent's level of education nor parental education level distinguish among the average number of content areas read or used within any category. Nevertheless, it should be noted that the trend within each category is in the expected direction, but no differences reach significance. In addition, and more important, these data do not address questions regarding the amount of time spent reading these materials or the quality of what is being read. Notwithstanding questions concerning the amount of time spent reading and the quality of the material read, this study reveals that most young adults have some literacy skills and choose to use them.

TABLE 11

Average Number of Content Areas Within Newspapers, and Different Magazines, Books and Brief Documents Read by Race/Ethnicity, Educational Attainment, and Parental Education*

	Newspapers**	Magazines**	Books**	Brief Documents**
Race/Ethnicity				
White	5.8 (3.0)	2.5 (1.6)	2.9 (2.0)	15.6 (7.7)
Black	5.6 (3.2)	2.6 (1.6)	2.3 (1.9)	12.1 (7.6)
Hispanic	5.7 (3.2)	2.4 (1.7)	2.3 (1.9)	13.8 (7.9)
Educational Attainment				
Less than high school	2.8 (3.2)	1.6 (1.3)	1.4 (1.7)	7.9 (5.9)
Some high school	4.7 (3.0)	2.0 (1.6)	1.4 (1.4)	8.8 (5.7)
High school graduate and/or some postsecondary	5.5 (3.0)	2.4 (1.6)	2.3 (1.8)	13.8 (7.1)
Postsecondary degree	6.6 (2.9)	2.9 (1.6)	4.0 (1.8)	19.0 (7.2)
Parental Education				
Less than high school	4.6 (3.4)	2.0 (1.6)	1.8 (1.6)	11.0 (7.0)
Some high school	4.8 (3.0)	2.1 (1.5)	1.9 (1.8)	11.0 (6.3)
High school graduate and/or some postsecondary	5.8 (3.1)	2.5 (1.6)	2.7 (1.9)	14.9 (7.4)
Postsecondary degree	6.3 (2.8)	2.9 (1.6)	3.6 (2.0)	18.0 (7.6)
Total	5.6 (3.1)	2.5 (1.6)	2.6 (2.0)	14.2 (7.8)

*Figures in parentheses are standard deviations.
**Range: Newspapers — 0 to 13
  Magazines — 0 to 5+
  Books — 0 to 7
  Brief Documents — 0 to 36

Section 4

Explaining Levels of Literacy

The characteristics of America's young adults are important in the clues they seem to provide toward understanding the various levels of literacy found within this population. These clues are incomplete, however, and can sometimes lead to a wrong conclusion since the variables measured do not operate in isolation but interact in complicated ways with performance. This section of the report summarizes one attempt to unravel these complex relationships.

A model was developed to address six major questions:

▶ Which background characteristics (racial/ethnic group membership, sex, parental education/occupation, and age at which the respondent learned to speak English) relate to the reported availability of literacy materials in the home?

▶ How do these particular background characteristics combine with availability of literacy materials in the home to predict choice of a high school curriculum (College Preparatory, General, Vocational) and young adults' levels of educational attainment?

▶ What are the most influential variables from the individual's background (including literacy materials in the home, choice of a high school curriculum and educational attainment) in predicting reported literacy practices and television viewing (hours per day spent watching TV)?

▶ How does the complete set of variables relate to estimated performance on the four proficiency measures — prose, document, and quantitative literacy scales, and the NAEP reading scale?

▶ Other things being equal, do the different literacy practices have varying impacts on achievement across the four proficiency measures?

▶ Does the pattern of relationships among the variables differ for White, Black, and Hispanic young adults?

The data* reveal a modest degree of association between the set of background variables and the respondent's reported access to literacy materials in the home. The background variable contributing most to this association is parental level of education, followed by parental occupation. Sex and age at which the respondent learned to speak English do not significantly contribute to the variation in literacy materials in the home after these other background characteristics are taken into account. It is interesting to note that, after taking background characteristics into account, Hispanic young adults report having access to fewer literacy materials in the home than do White young adults. Black young adults' reported access to literacy materials, however, is about midway between their White and Hispanic peers and does not differ significantly from either group.

Parental education level and occupation along with access to literacy materials in the home are the most salient characteristics associated with whether or not the respondent participated in a college-preparatory program (choice of curriculum). After holding constant parental education, occupation, and access to literacy materials in the home, there are no significant differences between males and females or among racial/ethnic groups in choice of a high school curriculum. Among Hispanic young adults, however, men appear more likely to choose a college-preparatory curriculum than are women.

The same characteristics — parental education and occupation along with access to literacy materials in the home — make a significant contribution to predicting the education level of young adults. Choice of high school curriculum, however, makes the largest contribution to predicting the respondent's level of education. This is not surprising, given the likelihood that individuals who do not, for whatever reasons, aspire to four-year or graduate-level degrees will be less likely to participate in a college-preparatory program.

Within the three racial/ethnic groups, literacy materials in the home and choice of high school curriculum contribute to the relationship with educational attainment. It is noteworthy that, once parental education and occupation are held constant, racial/ethnic group membership is not significantly associated with either choice of high school curriculum or the educational attainment of young adults.

The next question focuses on background and educational variables and the extent to which they relate to the reported use of brief documents, and the reading and/or use of newspapers, magazines, and books. With few exceptions, there is little difference between racial/ethnic groups and their reported literacy activities. As expected, the variables contributing most to the associations with these various literacy practices (newspapers, magazines, books, and brief documents) are: ac-

---

*The model and summary tables of analyses relating to each question are provided in the Final Report.

cess to literacy materials in the home, level of parental education, choice of a high school curriculum, and the respondent's level of education. The exceptions are that Black young adults report reading more magazines than do White young adults and White young adults report reading and/or using more brief documents than do Black young adults. It is not clear from the data whether the latter result stems more from a matter of choice or from the fact that brief documents are frequently associated with the workplace and technical training.

In contrast to literacy practices, racial/ethnic group membership has the strongest relationship with the amount of television that is reportedly watched each day. Black young adults watch more television each day than do either White or Hispanic young adults. Again, young adults' level of education, parental level of education and occupation, and age at which respondent learned English contribute significantly to the prediction of TV watching. Women report watching more television than do men, but this finding may simply reflect the fact that more women than men report staying at home.

The next question addresses the extent to which these background characteristics, educational variables, and literacy practices relate to the measures of literacy skills. The two variables that appear to have the strongest relationship to performance on each of the scales are racial/ethnic group membership and the respondent's level of education. But again, parental education contributes to the relationships.

In trying to better understand the relationships between these background variables and literacy proficiency, two findings stand out.

■ **After taking into account background and educational characteristics, the amount of time spent watching TV is not significantly related to performance on any of the proficiency scales.**

■ **Literacy practices relate to performance in different but expected ways. For example, using and reading books and newspapers relate significantly to the performance of these young adults on the NAEP reading scale, but it is the use and reading of books and brief documents that significantly relate to performance on the prose and document literacy scales. Newspaper reading relates to performance on all but the prose literacy scale.**

Accounting for Racial/Ethnic Differences

Another important question is to what extent the differences between racial/ethnic groups can be accounted for by these sets of background variables and characteristics. Table 12 gives the racial/ethnic group differences in terms of scale scores on each of the four proficiency measures, both before and after controlling for selected sets of background variables. Before applying any statistical controls, the average differences on the four scales between Black and White young adults range between 51 and 60 scale points. The average differences between Black and Hispanic young adults range from 21 to 27 scale points.

The first statistical control involves a set of demographic and background characteristics that includes sex, parental education and occupation, age at which the respondent learned English, and access to literacy materials in the home. Together, these variables explain about 20 percent or roughly 12 points of the average score differences between Black and White young adults on each of the four proficiency scales. The second statistical control involves adding the set of school variables (choice of a high school curriculum and educational attainment) to the set of demographic variables. A final set of statistical controls involves adding the set of literacy practices to the school and demographic variables. After these controls have been applied, the percentage of scale score differences accounted for increases to 27 percent or about 15 scale score points.

Average performance differences between Black and Hispanic young adults have a tendency to increase after the sets of background, education, and literacy practice variables are controlled. This probably reflects the fact that, on average, the Hispanic young adults reported coming from less advantageous environments than did Black young adults. That is, Hispanic young adults tended to report having fewer literacy materials in their homes while in high school and more parents having attained eight or fewer years of education.

TABLE 12
Differences Among Racial/Ethnic Groups on Each of the Proficiency Scales Before and After Holding Constant Background, Education, and Literacy Practice Variables*

Proficiency Scale	Scale Score Difference With No Statistical Controls		Scale Score Differences Remaining after Holding Constant Background/Demographics		Scale Score Differences Remaining After Holding Constant Demographics and Education		Scale Score Differences Remaining after Holding Constant Demographics, Education, and Literacy Practice	
	White (1)	Hispanic (2)	White (3)	Hispanic (4)	White (5)	Hispanic (6)	White (7)	Hispanic (8)
NAEP Reading	50.5	23.3	39.5	28.1	37.1	26.6	36.2	24.7
Prose	56.1	27.2	44.3	31.7	42.0	30.2	41.0	28.5
Document	60.0	23.0	48.2	29.4	45.5	27.8	44.3	25.6
Quantitative	55.1	21.2	44.1	25.4	41.7	24.0	40.0	21.1

*All contrasts are with the Black young adult sample. The entries in columns 1 and 2 indicate the average performance difference between that group and White and Hispanic young adults, respectively, before controlling for any variables. The first entry in Column 3 (39.5) indicates that, after controlling for demographics, White young adults, on average, score 39.5 points higher than their Black peers on the NAEP reading scale. Similarly, the first entry in column 6 indicates that the reading scores of Hispanic young adults are, on average, 26.6 points higher than those of their Black peers when demographics and education are statistically controlled.

Cautionary Note

The results from these relational analyses suggest, among other things, that the most promising intervention strategies are likely to be those that take into account the intergenerational aspects of poor academic performance — parental education, economic situation, and early home experiences are all likely to affect the individual's system of values and knowledge. These value and knowledge systems can be expected to have cumulative and lasting effects on interests, motivations and aspirations, and ultimately on literacy practices and proficiencies. It should be recognized that the variables used in these analyses are proxies for the more complex systems. As such, the proxy variables carry with them the effects of the more complex systems that are not measured directly. Therefore, simply adding more literacy materials to the home, for example, without stimulating their use *cannot* be expected to result in increased literacy proficiencies.

It is also important to note that the gaps between White, Black, and Hispanic young adults do not imply that minority group members score only at the lower levels on each of the literacy scales. In fact, roughly 20 percent of Black and approximately 35 percent of Hispanic young adults are estimated to be at or above the average proficiency level (305) on each of the scales. Moreover, some social scientists have argued that the gaps in socioeconomic status (SES) between, for example, White and Black populations appear to be more reflective of class than race differences per se. For example, data from High School and Beyond indicate that Black and Hispanic students are overrepresented in the low socioeconomic status group, which includes approximately 54 percent of Black and 57 percent of Hispanic high school seniors. The large deficits in academic skills found among high school seniors from low-SES backgrounds are consistently one standard deviation below the average scores of those students from high-SES backgrounds.*

*A. Sum, P. Harrington, and W. Goedicke. *Basic Skills of America's Teens and Young Adults: Findings of the 1980 National ASVAB Testing and Their Implications for Education, Employment and Training Policies and Programs.* Boston, MA: Center for Labor Market Studies, Northeastern University, 1986.

Section 5

Oral-Language Task Performance

A unique aspect of NAEP's young adult literacy assessment was the attempt to assess oral-language production. A set of 10 oral language tasks was administered to two groups: the one percent of the English-speaking young adults who were judged to have such limited literacy skills that they were not administered the set of simulation tasks — the "oral-language-only sample" — and a random subsample of the 98 percent of the English-speaking young adults who responded to the simulation tasks and for whom estimates of their proficiencies are given — the "simulation-task subsample." This provides an opportunity to look at the range of performance on the set of oral tasks for each of these two groups, as well as to compare their performances.

The Oral-Language Tasks

The oral-language tasks that were developed as part of NAEP's literacy assessment were thought to be appropriate for young men and women from all types of backgrounds and interests. They did not require special knowledge or prior preparation. Even though the tasks covered topics that almost everyone can talk about, they were constructed to represent different communication demands.

Two tasks thought to be among the least demanding require individuals to answer three questions about a photograph and to describe a sequence of events shown in a series of six photographs. A third exercise involves a basic but potentially important survival task — providing sufficient information to the fire department about a fire in the respondent's home. A fourth task requires giving directions to a local grocery store, while a fifth asks respondents to describe a movie or a television show. Two additional tasks attempt to elicit persuasive communication. One is personal and involves making an appeal to a prospective employer; the other is somewhat more abstract and requires stating one's opinion of increasing restrictions on smoking in public places. One other task, administered to everyone as part of the "core," involves having the respondents describe what they like to do in their spare time.

Scoring the Oral Tasks

Each of the oral tasks was tape recorded and returned to NAEP where evaluations were conducted by a team of scorers using guides that had been developed on the basis of actual responses.

Responses to each task were evaluated from four perspectives: (1) comprehensibility, (2) overall task accomplishment, (3) delivery problems, and (4) language problems. If a task was judged not comprehensible, the scoring ceased. The second rating was used to determine whether the speaker was "off task," or had provided a "minimal," "adequate," or "superior" response. The "superior" rating requires an elaborated response and was only used for the more demanding tasks. The third and fourth ratings, delivery and language, were used to identify problems that might contribute to low ratings in comprehensibility or task accomplishment.

A full description of the results of this phase of the assessment is provided in the Final Report on NAEP's assessment of young adults. In this report, the focus is on summarizing the results on the overall task-accomplishment rating, as well as relating selected background characteristics to oral-task performance.

Task Accomplishment

A summary of the task accomplishment results is presented in Figure 4. This figure shows the percentages of both the oral-language-only sample and the simulation-task subsample who provided an adequate or better response to each task.

Information in Figure 4 shows that on seven out of 10 oral tasks, at least 40 percent of the oral-language-only sample received a task accomplishment rating of adequate or better. Moreover, on three out of the 10 tasks, 70 percent or more of this group received an adequate or better rating. On the other hand, the results show that on all tasks, the simulation-task subsample outperform the oral-language-only sample. These differences reached statistical significance on seven of the 10 oral tasks. Two of the three tasks for which there were no significant differences between the groups were found to be relatively easy for everyone. These involved looking at a picture of a woman holding a tire and standing next to a car that has been jacked up. Responses were obtained to the questions: "What happened?" and "What will happen next?" In contrast, the third task for which no differences were found was extremely difficult for everyone. This task asked the speaker to give directions to get to a local grocery store. The difficulty of this task probably relates to the requirements of the scoring guide as much as the specific demands of the task.

Figure 4

PERCENTAGE OF YOUNG ADULTS WITH ADEQUATE OR BETTER ORAL-TASK ACCOMPLISHMENT RATING †

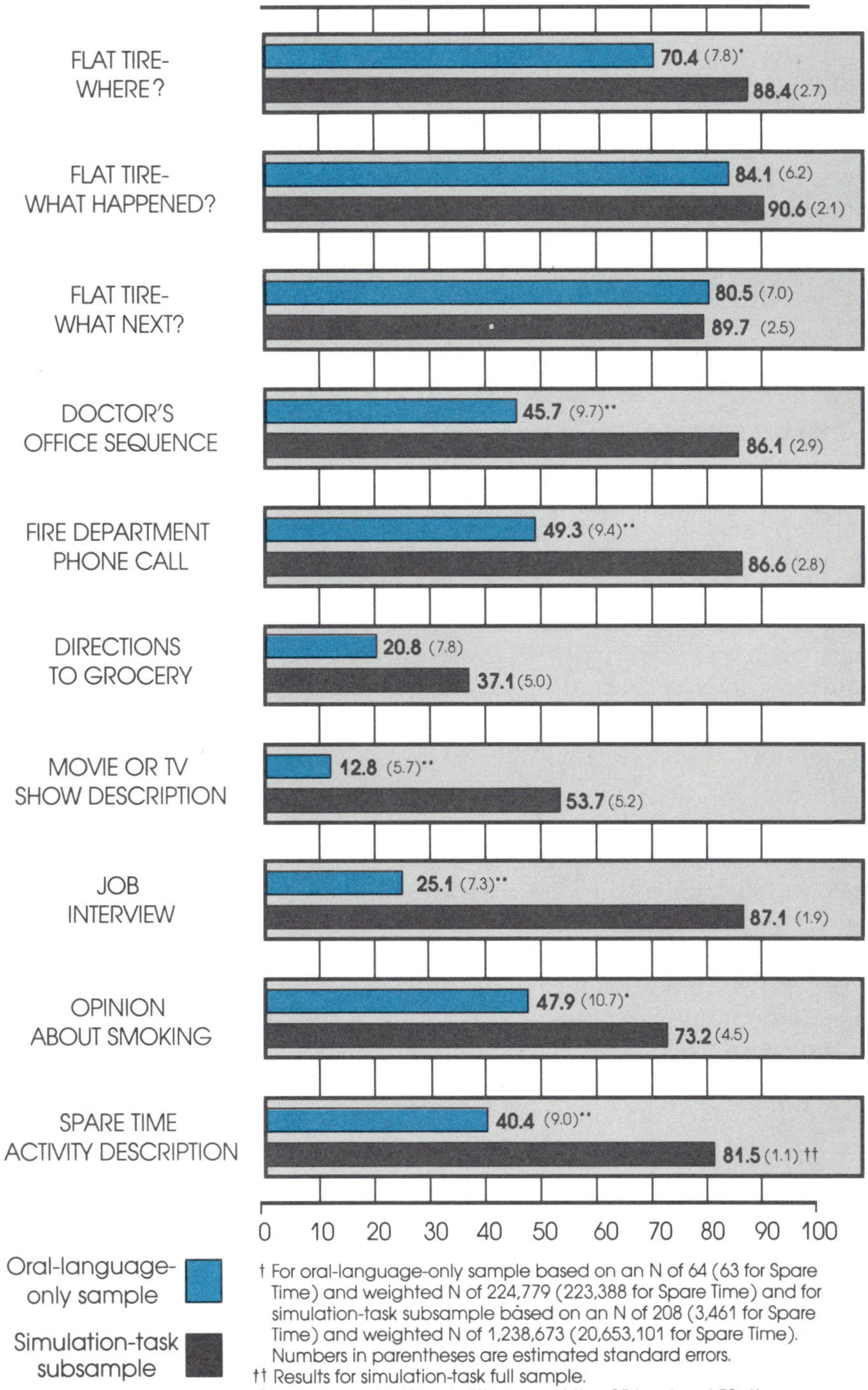

Task	Oral-language-only sample	Simulation-task subsample
FLAT TIRE- WHERE?	70.4 (7.8)*	88.4 (2.7)
FLAT TIRE- WHAT HAPPENED?	84.1 (6.2)	90.6 (2.1)
FLAT TIRE- WHAT NEXT?	80.5 (7.0)	89.7 (2.5)
DOCTOR'S OFFICE SEQUENCE	45.7 (9.7)**	86.1 (2.9)
FIRE DEPARTMENT PHONE CALL	49.3 (9.4)**	86.6 (2.8)
DIRECTIONS TO GROCERY	20.8 (7.8)	37.1 (5.0)
MOVIE OR TV SHOW DESCRIPTION	12.8 (5.7)**	53.7 (5.2)
JOB INTERVIEW	25.1 (7.3)**	87.1 (1.9)
OPINION ABOUT SMOKING	47.9 (10.7)*	73.2 (4.5)
SPARE TIME ACTIVITY DESCRIPTION	40.4 (9.0)**	81.5 (1.1) ††

† For oral-language-only sample based on an N of 64 (63 for Spare Time) and weighted N of 224,779 (223,388 for Spare Time) and for simulation-task subsample based on an N of 208 (3,461 for Spare Time) and weighted N of 1,238,673 (20,653,101 for Spare Time). Numbers in parentheses are estimated standard errors.
†† Results for simulation-task full sample.
* Statistically significant difference at the .05 level and 50 df.
** Statistically significant difference at the .005 level and 50 df.

Background Characteristics

Some of the differences in performance between the two groups may be associated with differences in background characteristics. While the sample sizes are relatively small, comparisons of the two groups can suggest factors that may play an important role in performance.

Members of the oral-language-only sample, as compared with the simulation task subsample, are more likely to be male, from a minority group, from a family in which a language other than English was spoken in the home, and from a family having less formal education. They are also more likely to have less education themselves, have a lower paying/lower status job, and have smaller household income. These data seem to call into question the view that "illiterate" adults have strong oral-language skills which, when combined with basic decoding skills will allow them to easily cross the threshold of print.

Relating Oral-Task Performance to the Proficiency Scales

A natural extension of this oral-language investigation is to examine the relationships between average performance across the oral-language tasks and performance on the four proficiency scales. This can be accomplished by looking at these relationships for the simulation-task subsample on average performance across the 10 tasks. This average was then correlated with performance on each of the literacy scales and on the NAEP reading scale. The relationships between the oral tasks and the proficiency scales are low to moderate (ranging from .33 to .38) and statistically significant.

In sum, these results suggest that there is a tendency for individuals who demonstrated limited literacy proficiency to also demonstrate restricted oral-language skills. Similarly, those who demonstrate higher levels of literacy also tend to demonstrate higher levels of performance on the oral-language tasks. Moreover, performance among the simulation-task subsample suggests that some persons within this group also have difficulty performing some of the tasks used in the oral-language assessment. Background data indicate that the oral-language-only sample was more likely to come from homes in which a language other than English was spoken and from lower socioeconomic and more limited educational backgrounds.

Section 6

Summary and Conclusions

Characterizing America as an "illiterate nation" is a little like characterizing America as a "diseased nation." Although millions suffer each year from debilitating illnesses, as a nation we are living longer and healthier lives than ever before. Similarly, although some of our citizens reach adulthood unable to read and write, we are a better educated and more literate society than at any time in our history.

Indeed, as Thomas Sticht points out in his foreword to this volume, NAEP's assessment of the literacy skills and strategies of young adults aged 21 to 25 years clearly indicates that the vast majority are literate according to standards applied by some scholars and historians. Virtually all young adults today demonstrate the ability to sign their name, thus making them literate according to standards applied to information available more than 100 years ago. Roughly 95 percent of the young adults reach or surpass the level of reading typical of the average fourth grader — the fourth grade being the standard adopted by the military almost half a century ago. By more recent standards, 80 percent of young adults are estimated to read as well as or better than the average eighth-grade student and more than 60 percent are estimated to read as well or better than the average eleventh-grade student.

An important question facing the nation is whether such simplistic standards adequately capture the broad and complex nature of literacy tasks encountered in today's society. The perspective taken in this assessment rejects these prior tests of literacy in favor of an approach that explicitly provides a means for understanding the various types and levels of literacy attained by young adults. The result is a more accurate representation not only of the complex information-processing demands found within a pluralistic society, but also of the range of skills and strategies that individuals demonstrate.

A large pool of "simulation tasks" was developed and administered by trained interviewers to a nationally representative sample of young adults residing in households in the contiguous 48 states. The literacy skills of this population were profiled in terms of:

- **prose literacy — skills and strategies needed to understand and use information from texts that are frequently found in the home or the community;**
- **document literacy — skills and strategies required to locate and use information contained in nontextual materials that include tables, graphs, charts, indexes, forms, and schedules;**
- **quantitative literacy — knowledge and skills needed to apply the arithmetic operations of addition, subtraction, multiplication, and division (either singly or sequentially) in combination with printed materials, as in balancing a checkbook or completing an order form.**

In addition, the assessment included a selected set of exercises from the 1983-84 NAEP reading assessment to link the performance of young adults to that of the in-school population.

Tasks representative of these types of literacy were placed on scales ranging from 0 to 500 with an average performance of 305. Most young adults were estimated to be proficient on tasks represented at the lower end of each scale, and more than half were estimated to have attained moderate levels of proficiency on each of the four scales. Nevertheless, relatively few young adults were estimated to have reached levels of proficiencies associated with the most complex and demanding tasks. While discussions of the distributions of group performance are instructive, they are somewhat empty without additional information to help interpret them.

Supplementary information to help interpret the literacy scales was developed by selecting tasks representative of various points along each of the scales and identifying the underlying characteristics contributing to task difficulty. For example, the 200 level on the prose scale is characterized by matching a single feature from a question to text material and also by producing text using personal background information. Tasks characterizing the 200 level on the document scale also require matching a single feature when no competing information in the document serves to distract the reader. A slightly more difficult task characterizes the lowest level on the quantitative scale. This task requires the reader to apply simple addition to information given.

Tasks at the more moderate levels of 275 to 325 on each of the scales engage the reader in relatively complex information-processing demands. For example, on the prose scale, such tasks require matching information on the basis of more than one feature, generalizing a familiar theme from text repeating a single idea, and interpreting materials such as a warranty. On the document scale, this range of difficulty is characterized by matching information on the basis of two or three features using graphic or tabular materials. This range of difficulty on the quantitative scale is characterized by tasks that require the reader to transfer and enter appropriate numerical information in combination with carrying out an arithmetic operation.

Increasingly more demanding tasks characterize higher levels on the literacy proficiency scales. On the prose scale, such tasks require matching information from complex and lengthy texts, generating a theme from a single unfamiliar metaphor, and interpreting the difference between two related statements. Tasks characteristic of the higher levels of the document scale involve matching information on as many as six features using a schedule that provides numerous pieces of information serving as distractors. On the quantitative scale, the more difficult tasks involve applying more than one numerical operation in the appropriate sequence on the basis of information that is frequently embedded in printed materials.

What these analyses suggest is that, in many instances, literacy tasks require individuals to apply complex information-processing skills and strategies. Some tasks require the reader to identify needed information, locate that information in a given source, remember it, combine it with additional information, and enter it onto a form or separate document. An example of such a task asks the reader to find information on a credit-card bill and use that information, along with other knowledge, to write a letter to the credit company explaining that a billing error has been made.

Awareness of these complex skills and strategies deepens our understanding about the nature of literacy in our society. Difficulties associated with employing these skills and strategies characterize the literacy problem for much of the young adult population, not "illiteracy" or the inability to decode print or comprehend simple textual materials.

While the information-processing analyses provide illuminating information regarding important aspects of the literacy problem for America's young adults, examination of the percentages of various groups that are estimated to have attained particular levels furthers our knowledge about the location and extent of the problem. For example, this assessment finds that White young adults surpass minority groups beginning at the 200 level on each of the scales and these differences increase in magnitude at succeeding levels. More than 95 percent of White, 90 percent of Hispanic, and 82 percent of Black young adults are estimated to be at or above the 200 level. However, by the 275 level, the percentages decrease to 78 percent of White and roughly 57 percent of Hispanic and 39 percent of Black young adults. By the 350 level, the percentages drop sharply for each group while the magnitude of the differences increases — approximately 25 percent of White, 10 percent of Hispanic, and just under 3 percent of Black young adults are estimated to attain or surpass this level.

As with differences among the racial/ethnic groups, those for respondents' reported levels of education are large and increase in magnitude at successive points along each of the scales. For example, 84 percent of persons with some high school experience, 97 percent of those who graduated from high school and/or have some postsecondary experience, and 99 percent of those earning postsecondary degrees are estimated to be at or above the 200 level on each of the scales. Again, discrepancies among groups differing in educational attainment become more pronounced by about the 275 level. Less than 30 percent of those reporting 0 to 8 years of education reach or surpass this 275 level. The percentage increases to 40 percent for those with some high school experience, rises to 68 percent for those with high school diplomas and/or some postsecondary experience, and reaches 91 percent for those earning postsecondary degrees. By the 350 level the decrease in percentages of each group are even more dramatic. Here, only 40 percent of those earning postsecondary degrees are estimated to be at or above the 350 level while only 12 percent of those with high school diplomas and/or some postsecondary experience, less than 4 percent of those reporting some high school experience, and less than 1 percent of those with 0 to 8 years of education achieve this or higher levels.

Minority group members as well as those persons who have terminated their education at an early point are disproportionately underrepresented at these middle- and high-proficiency levels. These findings, while disturbing in and of themselves, take on increased importance in light of the changing patterns of demographics projected for the young adult population. Within the next decade, it is expected that the total number of young adults aged 21 to 25 will shrink from around 21 million to roughly 17 million and will be comprised of increasing proportions of minorities. If these population estimates are accurate, there will be a less literate pool of Americans from which colleges, universities, industry, and the military will be able to draw to meet their human resource needs. This will occur unless appropriate intervention strategies are developed and implemented to meet the diverse needs of current young adults as well as to promote higher proficiencies among the younger, school-aged populations.

In addition, this study reveals that a small percentage of these young adults are among the least literate adults in America. Contributing to their difficulties is the fact that they tend to be lower in performance on the oral-language tasks as well. This suggests that longer and perhaps different types of programs will be needed for these individuals to make significant improvements in their language and literacy skills.

Some have argued that as the nation moves from an industrial to an information-service economy, many if not most of the managerial, technical, and professional jobs will require individuals to participate in additional training and education. Coordinated efforts seem to be needed both to develop and to apply appropriate intervention strategies that will allow individuals to take advantage of their existing skill levels in upgrading their proficiencies. Such programs should also be aimed at expanding the percentages of those in our population who are able to perform some of society's most complex tasks. Such strategies may serve not only to benefit the existing population of young adults who are or may become parents, but may also serve to improve opportunities for future generations of children.

To the extent that the skills identified in this literacy assessment are important for full participation in our society, this study raises some important issues. Should we seek better ways to teach the current curriculum or do we need to reconsider what is taught and how we teach it? Adult literacy programs aimed at developing comprehension skills are frequently based on elementary school reading models that, for the most part, are restricted to the use of narrative texts. Results from this and other studies suggest that primary emphases on a single aspect of literacy may not lead to the acquisition of the complex information-processing skills and strategies needed to cope successfully with the broad array of tasks adults face.

Other adult literacy programs that tend to focus on the acquisition of skills associated with discrete tasks, such as filling out a job application form or using a bus schedule, may have limited impact for the individual. This may be so because, while literacy is not a single skill suited to all types of texts, neither is it an infinite number of isolated skills each associated with a given type of text or document. Rather, as this assessment shows, there may well be an ordered set of information-processing skills and strategies that may be called into play to accomplish the range of tasks represented in the various aspects of literacy as defined here.

As one final point, becoming fully literate in a technologically advanced society is a lifelong pursuit, as is sustaining good health. Both are complex and depend upon a number of factors. So, just as there is no single action or step, that if taken, will ensure the physical health of every individual, there is no single action or step, that if taken, will ensure that every individual will become fully literate.

Authors' Acknowledgements

The responsibility for this document is ours. Nevertheless, credit, if any should accrue, must be shared with the many individuals who contribute to a project of this size and scope. These individuals range from the consultants who generously gave their thoughts and ideas to those who designed, printed, and shipped assessment materials to the more than 500 interviewers across the country; to Response Analysis Corporation, which was responsible for the field work; to the 3,600 young adults who participated in the assessment; to those who received, scored, entered, and produced the data tape; to those who analyzed the data; and, to those who provided expert opinions in interpreting the findings.

Some, because of their particular contribution to this assessment, are named here: Jan Applebaum, Laurie Barnett, John Barone, Albert Beaton, Marylou Bennett, Anne Campbell, David Freund, Jules Goodison, Bruce Kaplan, Edward Kulick, Barbara McQuaide, Ina Mullis, Norma Norris, Judith Pollack, Kathy Sheehan, Peter Stremic, and John Woloson.

We would also like to thank those individuals who provided thoughtful and incisive comments on early drafts of both the Final Report and this document. Included are: Kent Ashworth, Paul Barton, Robert Glaser, Margaret Goertz, Carl Kaestle, Archie Lapointe, Robert Linn, Samuel Messick, Andrew Sum, Donald Trismen, William Turnbull, and Richard Venezky.

Thomas Sticht not only reviewed our words and thoughts but also contributed in a special way by writing the foreword to this document. Jack Weaver's unique talents are apparent throughout this report but most notably in his watercolor interpretation of the study, reproduced on the cover.

We appreciate both the support and interest of members of the staff of the Office of Educational Research and Improvement. We are especially grateful to Maureen Treacy, who in her role as Project Monitor facilitated the conduct of the study and provided the professionalism and trust necessary to carry out a project of this type.

Darlene Wene deserves special recognition not only for careful preparation of the manuscripts in their various versions, but also for her spirit and good nature in accomplishing this work.

On a more personal note, we would like to express our warmest appreciation to Robert Mislevy, Peter Mosenthal, and Donald Rock, both for the generosity with which they shared their knowledge and ideas and for the friendships that resulted.

Finally, a great deal of expertise was brought to bear in developing this assessment and in reporting the results. We have learned a great deal in the process and hope that we have been able to share some of this knowledge and the accompanying insights in this report.

IK and AJ